Timed Readings Plus *in Science*

25 Two-Part Lessons
with Questions for
Building Reading Speed and Comprehension

BOOK 8

New York, New York   Columbus, Ohio   Chicago, Illinois   Peoria, Illinois   Woodland Hills, California

JAMESTOWN  EDUCATION

Glencoe/McGraw-Hill
A Division of The *McGraw·Hill* Companies

ISBN: 0-07-827377-3

Copyright © The McGraw-Hill Companies, Inc. All rights reserved. Except as permitted under the United States Copyright Act of 1976, no part of this publication may be reproduced or distributed in any form or by any means, or stored in a database or retrieval system, without prior written permission of the publisher.

Send all queries to:
Glencoe/McGraw-Hill
8787 Orion Place
Columbus, OH 43240-4027

1 2 3 4 5 6 7 8 9 10   021   08 07 06 05 04 03 02

CONTENTS

To the Student

    Reading Faster and Better   2

    Mastering Reading Comprehension   3

    Working Through a Lesson   7

    Plotting Your Progress   8

To the Teacher

    About the Series   9

    Timed Reading and Comprehension   10

    Speed Versus Comprehension   10

    Getting Started   10

    Timing the Reading   11

    Teaching a Lesson   11

    Monitoring Progress   12

    Diagnosis and Evaluation   12

Lessons   13–112

Answer Key   114–115

Graphs   116–118

To the Student

You probably talk at an average rate of about 150 words a minute. If you are a reader of average ability, you read at a rate of about 250 words a minute. So your reading speed is nearly twice as fast as your speaking or listening speed. This example shows that reading is one of the fastest ways to get information.

The purpose of this book is to help you increase your reading rate and understand what you read. The 25 lessons in this book will also give you practice in reading science articles and in preparing for tests in which you must read and understand nonfiction passages within a certain time limit.

Reading Faster and Better

Following are some strategies that you can use to read the articles in each lesson.

Previewing

Previewing before you read is a very important step. This helps you to get an idea of what a selection is about and to recall any previous knowledge you have about the subject. Here are the steps to follow when previewing.

Read the title. Titles are designed not only to announce the subject but also to make the reader think. Ask yourself questions such as What can I learn from the title? What thoughts does it bring to mind? What do I already know about this subject?

Read the first sentence. If they are short, read the first two sentences. The opening sentence is the writer's opportunity to get your attention. Some writers announce what they hope to tell you in the selection. Some writers state their purpose for writing; others just try to get your attention.

Read the last sentence. If it is short, read the final two sentences. The closing sentence is the writer's last chance to get ideas across to you. Some writers repeat the main idea once more. Some writers draw a conclusion—this is what they have been leading up to. Other writers summarize their thoughts; they tie all the facts together.

Skim the entire selection. Glance through the selection quickly to see what other information you can pick up. Look for anything that will help you read fluently and with understanding. Are there names, dates, or numbers? If so, you may have to read more slowly.

Reading for Meaning

Here are some ways to make sure you are making sense of what you read.

Build your concentration. You cannot understand what you read if you are not concentrating. When you discover that your thoughts are straying, correct the situation right away. Avoid distractions and distracting situations. Keep in mind the information you learned from previewing. This will help focus your attention on the selection.

Read in thought groups. Try to see meaningful combinations of words—phrases, clauses, or sentences. If you look at only one word at a time (called word-by-word reading), both your comprehension and your reading speed suffer.

Ask yourself questions. To sustain the pace you have set for yourself and to maintain a high level of concentration and comprehension, ask yourself questions such as What does this mean? or How can I use this information? as you read.

Finding the Main Ideas

The paragraph is the basic unit of meaning. If you can quickly discover and understand the main idea of each paragraph, you will build your comprehension of the selection.

Find the topic sentence. The topic sentence, which contains the main idea, often is the first sentence of a paragraph. It is followed by sentences that support, develop, or explain the main idea. Sometimes a topic sentence comes at the end of a paragraph. When it does, the supporting details come first, building the base for the topic sentence. Some paragraphs do not have a topic sentence; all of the sentences combine to create a meaningful idea.

Understand paragraph structure. Every well-written paragraph has a purpose. The purpose may be to inform, define, explain or illustrate. The purpose should always relate to the main idea and expand on it. As you read each paragraph, see how the body of the paragraph tells you more about the main idea.

Relate ideas as you read. As you read the selection, notice how the writer puts together ideas. As you discover the relationship between the ideas, the main ideas come through quickly and clearly.

Mastering Reading Comprehension

Reading fast is not useful if you don't remember or understand what you read. The two exercises in Part A provide a check on how well you have understood the article.

Recalling Facts

These multiple-choice questions provide a quick check to see how well you recall important information from the article. As you learn to apply the reading strategies described earlier, you should be able to answer these questions more successfully.

Understanding Ideas

These questions require you to think about the main ideas in the article. Some main ideas are stated in the article; others are not. To answer some of the questions, you need to draw conclusions about what you read.

The five exercises in Part B require multiple answers. These exercises provide practice in applying comprehension and critical thinking skills that you can use in all your reading.

Recognizing Words in Context

Always check to see whether the words around an unfamiliar word—its context—can give you a clue to the word's meaning. A word generally appears in a context related to its meaning.

Suppose, for example, that you are unsure of the meaning of the word *expired* in the following passage:

> Vera wanted to check out a book, but her library card had expired. She had to borrow my card, because she didn't have time to renew hers.

You could begin to figure out the meaning of *expired* by asking yourself a question such as, What could have happened to Vera's library card that would make her need to borrow someone else's card? You might realize that if Vera had to renew her card, its usefulness must have come to an end or run out. This would lead you to conclude that the word *expired* must mean "to come to an end" or "to run out." You would be right. The context suggested the meaning.

Context can also affect the meaning of a word you already know. The word *key*, for instance, has many meanings. There are musical keys, door keys, and keys to solving a mystery. The context in which the word *key* occurs will tell you which meaning is correct.

Sometimes a word is explained by the words that immediately follow it. The subject of a sentence and your knowledge about that subject might also help you determine the meaning of an unknown word. Try to decide the meaning of the word *revive* in the following sentence:

> Sunshine and water will revive those drooping plants.

The compound subject is *sunshine* and *water*. You know that plants need light and water to survive and that drooping plants are not healthy. You can figure out that *revive* means "to bring back to health."

Distinguishing Fact from Opinion

Every day you are called upon to sort out fact and opinion. Because much of what you read and hear contains both facts and opinions, you need to be able to tell the two apart.

Facts are statements that can be proved true. The proof must be objective and verifiable. You must be able to check for yourself to confirm a fact.

Look at the following facts. Notice that they can be checked for accuracy and confirmed. Suggested sources for verification appear in parentheses.

- Abraham Lincoln was the 16th president of the United States. (Consult biographies, social studies books, encyclopedias, and similar sources.)

- Earth revolves around the Sun. (Research in encyclopedias or astronomy books; ask knowledgeable people.)
- Dogs walk on four legs. (See for yourself.)

Opinions are statements that cannot be proved true. There is no objective evidence you can consult to check the truthfulness of an opinion. Unlike facts, opinions express personal beliefs or judgments. Opinions reveal how someone feels about a subject, not the facts about that subject. You might agree or disagree with someone's opinion, but you cannot prove it right or wrong.

Look at the following opinions. The reasons these statements are classified as opinions appear in parentheses.

- Abraham Lincoln was born to be a president. (You cannot prove this by referring to birth records. There is no evidence to support this belief.)
- Earth is the only planet in our solar system where intelligent life exists. (There is no proof of this. It may be proved true some day, but for now it is just an educated guess—not a fact.)
- The dog is a human's best friend. (This is not a fact; your best friend might not be a dog.)

As you read, be aware that facts and opinions are often mixed together. Both are useful to you as a reader. But to evaluate what you read and to read intelligently, you need to know the difference between the two.

Keeping Events in Order

Sequence, or chronological order, is the order of events in a story or article or the order of steps in a process. Paying attention to the sequence of events or steps will help you follow what is happening, predict what might happen next, and make sense of a passage.

To make the sequence as clear as possible, writers often use signal words to help the reader get a more exact idea of when things happen. Following is a list of frequently used signal words and phrases:

until	first
next	then
before	after
finally	later
when	while
during	now
at the end	by the time
as soon as	in the beginning

Signal words and phrases are also useful when a writer chooses to relate details or events out of sequence. You need to pay careful attention to determine the correct chronological order.

Making Correct Inferences

Much of what you read *suggests* more than it *says*. Writers often do not state ideas directly in a text. They can't. Think of the time and space it would take to state every idea. And think of how boring that would be! Instead, writers leave it to you, the reader, to fill in the information they leave out—to make inferences. You do this by combining clues in the story or article with knowledge from your own experience.

You make many inferences every day. Suppose, for example, that you are visiting a friend's house for the first time. You see a bag of kitty litter. You infer (make an inference) that the family has a cat. Another day you overhear a conversation. You catch the names of two actors and the words *scene, dialogue,* and *directing*. You infer that the people are discussing a movie or play.

In these situations and others like them, you infer unstated information from what you observe or read. Readers must make inferences in order to understand text.

Be careful about the inferences you make. One set of facts may suggest several inferences. Some of these inferences could be faulty. A correct inference must be supported by evidence.

Remember that bag of kitty litter that caused you to infer that your friend has a cat? That could be a faulty inference. Perhaps your friend's family uses the kitty litter on their icy sidewalks to create traction. To be sure your inference is correct, you need more evidence.

Understanding Main Ideas

The main idea is the most important idea in a paragraph or passage—the idea that provides purpose and direction. The rest of the selection explains, develops, or supports the main idea. Without a main idea, there would be only a collection of unconnected thoughts.

In the following paragraph, the main idea is printed in italics. As you read, observe how the other sentences develop or explain the main idea.

Typhoon Chris hit with full fury today on the central coast of Japan. Heavy rain from the storm flooded the area. High waves carried many homes into the sea. People now fear that the heavy rains will cause mudslides in the central part of the country. The number of people killed by the storm may climb past the 200 mark by Saturday.

In this paragraph, the main-idea statement appears first. It is followed by sentences that explain, support, or give details. Sometimes the main idea appears at the end of a paragraph. Writers often put the main idea at the end of a paragraph when their purpose is to persuade or convince. Readers may be more open to a new idea if the reasons for it are presented first.

As you read the following paragraph, think about the overall impact of the supporting ideas. Their purpose is to convince the reader that the main idea in the last sentence should be accepted.

Last week there was a head-on collision at Huntington and Canton streets. Just a month ago a pedestrian was struck there. Fortunately, she was only slightly injured. In the past year, there have been more accidents there than at any other corner in the city. In fact, nearly 10 percent of all accidents in the city occur at the corner. This intersection is very dangerous, and a traffic signal should be installed there before a life is lost.

The details in the paragraph progress from least important to most important. They achieve their full effect in the main idea statement at the end.

In many cases, the main idea is not expressed in a single sentence. The reader is called upon to interpret all of the ideas expressed in the paragraph and to decide upon a main idea. Read the following paragraph.

> The American author Jack London was once a pupil at the Cole Grammar School in Oakland, California. Each morning the class sang a song. When the teacher noticed that Jack wouldn't sing, she sent him to the principal. He returned to class with a note. The note said that Jack could be excused from singing with the class if he would write an essay every morning.

In this paragraph, the reader has to interpret the individual ideas and to decide on a main idea. This main idea seems reasonable: Jack London's career as a writer began with a punishment in grammar school.

Understanding the concept of the main idea and knowing how to find it is important. Transferring that understanding to your reading and study is also important.

Working Through a Lesson

Part A

1. **Preview the article.** Locate the timed selection in Part A of the lesson that you are going to read. Wait for your teacher's signal to preview. You will have 20 seconds for previewing. Follow the previewing steps described on page 2.

2. **Read the article.** When your teacher gives you the signal, begin reading. Read carefully so that you will be able to answer questions about what you have read. When you finish reading, look at the board and note your reading time. Write this time at the bottom of the page on the line labeled Reading Time.

3. **Complete the exercises.** Answer the 10 questions that follow the article. There are 5 fact questions and 5 idea questions. Choose the best answer to each question and put an X in that box.

4. **Correct your work.** Use the Answer Key at the back of the book to check your answers. Circle any wrong answer and put an X in the box you should have marked. Record the number of correct answers on the appropriate line at the end of the lesson.

Part B

1. **Preview and read the passage.** Use the same techniques you

used to read Part A. Think about what you are reading.

2. **Complete the exercises.** Instructions are given for answering each category of question. There are 15 responses for you to record.

3. **Correct your work.** Use the Answer Key at the back of the book. Circle any wrong answer and write the correct letter or number next to it. Record the number of correct answers on the appropriate line at the end of the lesson.

Plotting Your Progress

1. **Find your reading rate.** Turn to the Reading Rate graph on page 116. Put an X at the point where the vertical line that represents the lesson intersects your reading time, shown along the left-hand side. The right-hand side of the graph will reveal your words-per-minute reading speed.

2. **Find your comprehension score.** Add your scores for Part A and Part B to determine your total number of correct answers. Turn to the Comprehension Score Graph on page 117. Put an X at the point where the vertical line that represents your lesson intersects your total correct answers, shown along the left-hand side. The right-hand side of the graph will show the percentage of questions you answered correctly.

3. **Complete the Comprehension Skills Profile.** Turn to page 118. Record your incorrect answers for the Part B exercises. The five Part B skills are listed along the bottom. There are five columns of boxes, one column for each question. For every incorrect answer, put an X in a box for that skill.

To get the most benefit from these lessons, you need to take charge of your own progress in improving your reading speed and comprehension. Studying these graphs will help you to see whether your reading rate is increasing and to determine what skills you need to work on. Your teacher will also review the graphs to check your progress.

TO THE TEACHER

About the Series

Timed Readings Plus in Science includes 10 books at reading levels 4–13, with one book at each level. Book One contains material at a fourth-grade reading level; Book Two at a fifth-grade level, and so on. The readability level is determined by the Fry Readability Scale and is not to be confused with grade or age level. The books are designed for use with students at middle school level and above.

The purposes of the series are as follows:

- to provide systematic, structured reading practice that helps students improve their reading rate and comprehension skills

- to give students practice in reading and understanding informational articles in the content area of science

- to give students experience in reading various text types—informational, expository, narrative, and prescriptive

- to prepare students for taking standardized tests that include timed reading passages in various content areas

- to provide materials with a wide range of reading levels so that students can continue to practice and improve their reading rate and comprehension skills

Because the books are designed for use with students at designated reading levels rather than in a particular grade, the science topics in this series are not correlated to any grade-level curriculum. Most standardized tests require students to read and comprehend science passages. This series provides an opportunity for students to become familiar with the particular requirements of reading science. For example, the vocabulary in a science article is important. Students need to know certain words in order to understand the concepts and the information.

Each book in the series contains 25 two-part lessons. Part A focuses on improving reading rate. This section of the lesson consists of a 400-word timed informational article on a science topic followed by two multiple-choice exercises. Recalling Facts includes five fact questions; Understanding Ideas includes five critical-thinking questions.

Part B concentrates on building mastery in critical areas of comprehension. This section consists of a nontimed passage—the "plus" passage—followed by five exercises that address five major comprehension skills. The passage varies in length; its subject matter relates to the content of the timed selection.

Timed Reading and Comprehension

Timed reading is the best-known method of improving reading speed. There is no point in someone's reading at an accelerated speed if the person does not understand what she or he is reading. Nothing is more important than comprehension in reading. The main purpose of reading is to gain knowledge and insight, to understand the information that the writer and the text are communicating.

Few students will be able to read a passage once and answer all of the questions correctly. A score of 70 or 80 percent correct is normal. If the student gets 90 or 100 percent correct, he or she is either reading too slowly or the material is at too low a reading level. A comprehension or critical thinking score of less than 70 percent indicates a need for improvement.

One method of improving comprehension and critical thinking skills is for the student to go back and study each incorrect answer. First, the student should reread the question carefully. It is surprising how many students get the wrong answer simply because they have not read the question carefully. Then the student should look back in the passage to find the place where the question is answered, reread that part of the passage, and think about how to arrive at the correct answer. It is important to be able to recognize a correct answer when it is embedded in the text. Teacher guidance or class discussion will help the student find an answer.

Speed Versus Comprehension

It is not unusual for comprehension scores to decline as reading rate increases during the early weeks of timed readings. If this happens, students should attempt to level off their speed—but not lower it—and concentrate more on comprehension. Usually, if students maintain the higher speed and concentrate on comprehension, scores will gradually improve and within a week or two be back up to normal levels of 70 to 80 percent.

It is important to achieve a proper balance between speed and comprehension. An inefficient reader typically reads everything at one speed, usually slowly. Some poor readers, however, read rapidly but without satisfactory comprehension. It is important to achieve a balance between speed and comprehension. The practice that this series provides enables students to increase their reading speed while maintaining normal levels of comprehension.

Getting Started

As a rule, the passages in a book designed to improve reading speed should be relatively easy. The student should not have much difficulty with the vocabulary or the subject matter. Don't worry about the passages being too easy; students should see how quickly and efficiently they can read a passage.

Begin by assigning students to a level. A student should start with a book that is one level below his or her current reading level. If a student's reading level is not known, a suitable starting point would be one or two levels below the student's present grade in school.

Introduce students to the contents and format of the book they are using. Examine the book to see how it is organized. Talk about the parts of each lesson. Discuss the purpose of timed reading and the use of the progress graphs at the back of the book.

Timing the Reading

One suggestion for timing the reading is to have all students begin reading the selection at the same time. After one minute, write on the board the time that has elapsed and begin updating it at 10-second intervals (1:00, 1:10, 1:20, etc.). Another option is to have individual students time themselves with a stopwatch.

Teaching a Lesson

Part A

1. Give students the signal to begin previewing the lesson. Allow 20 seconds, then discuss special science terms or vocabulary that students found.

2. Use one of the methods described above to time students as they read the passage. (Include the 20-second preview time as part of the first minute.) Tell students to write down the last time shown on the board or the stopwatch when they finish reading. Have them record the time in the designated space after the passage.

3. Next, have students complete the exercises in Part A. Work with them to check their answers, using the Answer Key that begins on page 114. Have them circle incorrect answers, mark the correct answers, and then record the numbers of correct answers for Part A on the appropriate line at the end of the lesson. Correct responses to eight or more questions indicate satisfactory comprehension and recall.

Part B

1. Have students read the Part B passage and complete the exercises that follow it. Directions are provided with each exercise. Correct responses require deliberation and discrimination.

2. Work with students to check their answers. Then discuss the answers with them and have them record the number of correct answers for Part B at the end of the lesson.

Have students study the correct answers to the questions they answered incorrectly. It is important that they understand why a particular answer is correct or incorrect.

Have them reread relevant parts of a passage to clarify an answer. An effective cooperative activity is to have students work in pairs to discuss their answers, explain why they chose the answers they did, and try to resolve differences.

Monitoring Progress

Have students find their total correct answers for the lesson and record their reading time and scores on the graphs on pages 116 and 117. Then have them complete the Comprehension Skills Profile on page 118. For each incorrect response to a question in Part B, students should mark an X in the box above each question type.

The legend on the Reading Rate graph automatically converts reading times to words-per-minute rates. The Comprehension Score graph automatically converts the raw scores to percentages.

These graphs provide a visual record of a student's progress. This record gives the student and you an opportunity to evaluate the student's progress and to determine the types of exercises and skills he or she needs to concentrate on.

Diagnosis and Evaluation

The following are typical reading rates.

Slow Reader—150 Words Per Minute

Average Reader—250 Words Per Minute

Fast Reader—350 Words Per Minute

A student who consistently reads at an average or above-average rate (with satisfactory comprehension) is ready to advance to the next book in the series.

A column of Xs in the Comprehension Skills Profile indicates a specific comprehension weakness. Using the profile, you can assess trends in student performance and suggest remedial work if necessary.

1 A   Eating for Good Health

When it comes to nutrition, people in the United States often make poor choices. Sometimes bad eating habits are not the consequence of a lack of nutritional information or the unavailability of nutritious foods; some people simply choose to eat poorly. They prefer to eat only the foods that taste delicious to them. Unfortunately, the decision to eat poorly has lasting consequences. As many as half of all Americans are overweight. Furthermore, many suffer from conditions such as heart disease, high blood pressure, and adult-onset diabetes that can result from these poor lifestyle choices. If we want to live long, healthy lives, we must make better nutritional decisions. Otherwise, we could be risking our health and our futures.

    Proper nutrition begins with knowledge. The United States Department of Agriculture (USDA) issues food guidelines to help people to make appropriate nutritional choices. These guidelines are summarized in a USDA chart called the Food Guide Pyramid. The Pyramid is based on research into the specific types of nutrients needed for disease resistance and proper body weight.

    According to the Pyramid, Americans should get most of their daily calorie intake from bread, cereal, rice, and pasta, eating 6 to 11 servings of these foods per day. Whole-grain products are the best. The larger numbers of servings are intended only for people such as athletes, whose work includes a great deal of physical activity. Following this category are the fruit and vegetable categories, with a total suggested consumption of from 5 to 9 servings per day. This emphasizes the importance of fiber, vitamins, and minerals in maintaining a healthy lifestyle. The Pyramid's other recommendations include 2 to 3 servings of dairy products and 2 to 3 servings from a group that includes meat, fish, beans, and nuts. The USDA recommends that fats and sweets be eaten sparingly.

    There are many risk factors that contribute to poor health. Among these are such lifestyle choices as improper nutrition and inadequate exercise. Current research by the American Heart Association shows that heart disease very often begins when a person is a child. Despite this, many Americans think they can postpone healthy eating and proper exercise until they have health problems. Unfortunately, diseases are not generally detected until symptoms begin, and by then it may be too late. To live long and productive lives, we must make proper choices now, including healthy nutritional choices.

Reading Time _____

Recalling Facts

1. The Food Guide Pyramid was developed by the
   - ❑ a. Department of Health and Human Services.
   - ❑ b. United States Department of Agriculture.
   - ❑ c. Centers for Disease Control.

2. The Food Guide Pyramid recommends that fats and sweets be eaten
   - ❑ a. once or twice a week.
   - ❑ b. between two and five times a day.
   - ❑ c. sparingly.

3. The approximate percentage of Americans who are overweight is
   - ❑ a. 25 percent.
   - ❑ b. 50 percent.
   - ❑ c. 70 percent.

4. The Food Guide Pyramid recommends the highest number of daily servings be in the _____ category.
   - ❑ a. fruits and vegetables
   - ❑ b. dairy products
   - ❑ c. bread, cereal, rice, and pasta

5. According to the American Heart Association, heart disease usually begins in
   - ❑ a. adolescence.
   - ❑ b. middle age.
   - ❑ c. childhood.

Understanding Ideas

6. This article suggests that poor nutrition can make a person
   - ❑ a. less intelligent.
   - ❑ b. more vulnerable to disease.
   - ❑ c. less attractive.

7. According to the article, the Food Guide Pyramid categorizes different food groups by the
   - ❑ a. number of calories in each.
   - ❑ b. grams of fat and cholesterol recommended per day.
   - ❑ c. number of recommended servings per day.

8. The USDA probably developed the Food Guide Pyramid to
   - ❑ a. help people choose foods for a well-balanced diet.
   - ❑ b. make people feel guilty about what they eat.
   - ❑ c. tell people what foods they should avoid.

9. You can conclude that fruits and vegetables are rich in
   - ❑ a. protein.
   - ❑ b. vitamins and minerals.
   - ❑ c. fat.

10. A middle-aged person who has been eating a diet high in fat since childhood probably has
    - ❑ a. a well-balanced diet.
    - ❑ b. some form of heart disease.
    - ❑ c. a low body weight.

1 B Nutritional Facts and Myths

Many people in the United States are obsessed with nutritional do's and don'ts. Magazines have articles in which people sing the praises of a new diet that has helped them lose lots of weight and feel great about themselves. On television, so-called experts are constantly recommending certain foods and warning about others. Sometimes they contradict one another! With certain items labeled "cancer cures" and others labeled "hazardous," it is difficult to know what to believe. Fortunately, the truth is not complicated. The passport to good health is not found in commercials or advertisements. Proper nutrition consists simply of eating a well-balanced diet.

Among nutritional myths are claims by "diet gurus" that you can lose weight and be healthier by eating special diets consisting of only two or three foods. It is almost impossible to get all of the necessary vitamins and nutrients from such a limited number of foods. Not getting enough of even one kind of vitamin over a period of days can lead to illness.

Another nutritional myth concerns protein intake. Protein is essential because it helps provide us with amino acids to build muscle, hair, and antibodies that fight foreign pathogens entering our systems. A popular myth is that we require a diet rich in meat to be healthy. This is simply not true, because many people in other countries are healthy despite eating little or no meat. Although meat is nutritious, large amounts of it are not necessary for a good diet.

1. **Recognizing Words in Context**

   Find the word *obsessed* in the passage. One definition below is closest to the meaning of that word. One definition has the opposite or nearly opposite meaning. The remaining definition has a completely different meaning. Label the definitions C for *closest*, O for *opposite or nearly opposite,* and D for *different.*

   _____ a. bored with

   _____ b. constantly eating

   _____ c. always thinking about

2. **Distinguishing Fact from Opinion**

   Two of the statements below present *facts*, which can be proved correct. The other statement is an *opinion*, which expresses someone's thoughts or beliefs. Label the statements F for *fact* and O for *opinion.*

   _____ a. Some information on nutrition is contradictory.

   _____ b. Protein is available from a number of sources.

   _____ c. Dieting is not an effective method of losing weight.

3. **Keeping Events in Order**

   Label the statements below 1, 2, and 3 to show the order in which the events happen.

   _____ a. A person began a diet of foods rich in protein.

   _____ b. A person read an article about a miracle protein-only diet.

   _____ c. A person's health worsened due to a lack of some vitamin.

4. **Making Correct Inferences**

   Two of the statements below are correct *inferences,* or reasonable guesses. They are based on information in the passage. The other statement is an incorrect, or faulty, inference. Label the statements C for *correct* inference and F for *faulty* inference.

   _____ a. Some diets can do more harm than good.

   _____ b. Only meat will supply us with the amino acids needed for good health.

   _____ c. Amino acids are required to build muscle tissue.

5. **Understanding Main Ideas**

   One of the statements below expresses the main idea of the passage. One statement is too general, or too broad. The other explains only part of the passage; it is too narrow. Label the statements M for *main idea,* B for *too broad,* and N for *too narrow.*

   _____ a. There are many nutritional facts and myths.

   _____ b. Meat is not the only good source of protein.

   _____ c. While there are many nutritional facts and myths, the best approach is to eat a well-balanced diet.

Correct Answers, Part A _____

Correct Answers, Part B _____

Total Correct Answers _____

2 A   Sea Mammals

Gliding through the sea, cetaceans fascinate people more than any other marine life. Cetaceans are sea mammals. They rule the ocean because of their cunning intelligence and their remarkable ability to communicate with each other in ways scientists are only beginning to understand. Gone are the days when humans could presume that their species was the only one with any intelligence. Now we are becoming more aware of the complex abilities cetaceans possess.

There are 77 known species of cetaceans, including whales, dolphins, and porpoises. Cetaceans exhibit a variety of behaviors. As scientists learn more about cetacean behavior, they are discovering that cetaceans and humans share an array of characteristics.

Like humans, cetaceans are mammals. All mammals have young that get milk from their mothers, have a backbone, have hair on their bodies, and are warm-blooded. Cetaceans have a large brain compared with non-mammals of the same size. They have a few hairs, such as whiskers, on their heads. Another trait humans and cetaceans share is their highly organized social structure. Cetaceans, too, live in large family units, called pods.

Another common feature is the cetaceans' ability to communicate with each other through sound waves. Although the process is not completely understood, it is known that cetaceans send and receive signals using a specialized method called echolocation. This is the emission and reception of sound waves. Scientists know cetaceans release sound, but they are uncertain where the sound comes from.

Many marine biologists think cetaceans release sound waves by thrusting and focusing their heads in certain directions. Still others theorize that sound waves are released through a larynx and focused by specialized sections in the skull. In contrast, there is no question how these animals receive sound waves. After being released, the cetaceans' echo passes through the water and is received by another of the same species through sound-conducting tissue located between the jawbone and inner ear. In this way, these animals share a distinctive language much as humans do.

Also like humans, cetaceans breathe oxygen. They do this by using a blowhole on their heads. Many cetaceans need to breathe only once every few minutes because their muscles can store large amounts of oxygen. At the surface, they exhale the gases that remain in their lungs, along with water vapor and other substances. This stream of vapor may shoot high into the air and be visible for long distances.

Reading Time _____

Recalling Facts

1. There are _____ known species of cetaceans.
   - ❏ a. 63
   - ❏ b. 77
   - ❏ c. 91

2. Cetaceans breathe
   - ❏ a. helium.
   - ❏ b. carbon monoxide.
   - ❏ c. oxygen.

3. The emission and reception of sound waves by cetaceans is known as
   - ❏ a. sonar.
   - ❏ b. hearing.
   - ❏ c. echolocation.

4. The sound-conducting tissue in cetaceans is located between their
   - ❏ a. jawbone and blowhole.
   - ❏ b. jawbone and inner ear.
   - ❏ c. brain and inner ear.

5. Like humans, cetaceans
   - ❏ a. have blowholes.
   - ❏ b. are cold blooded.
   - ❏ c. are mammals.

Understanding Ideas

6. What is a likely reason that humans must breathe more often than cetaceans?
   - ❏ a. Humans' muscles do not store oxygen as well.
   - ❏ b. Humans are not as skilled at survival.
   - ❏ c. Cetaceans do not require oxygen to live.

7. It is possible to conclude from the article that as we learn more about the complex nature of some creatures, we
   - ❏ a. learn to fear them.
   - ❏ b. gain an appreciation for them.
   - ❏ c. learn how to speak their language.

8. Which of the following would be one acceptable reason that sharks are not cetaceans?
   - ❏ a. They kill other animals.
   - ❏ b. The females do not provide milk to their young.
   - ❏ c. They rarely live in pods.

9. A characteristic of an intelligent species is the species' ability to
   - ❏ a. breathe oxygen.
   - ❏ b. hunt in packs.
   - ❏ c. communicate.

10. Communication, the breathing of oxygen, and a highly organized social structure characterize
    - ❏ a. both humans and cetaceans.
    - ❏ b. humans only.
    - ❏ c. cetaceans only.

2 B A Powerful Killer

The killer whale, whose scientific name is *Orcinus orca*, is often perceived as a menacing force and a ruthless killer. This animal is actually a member of the dolphin family. Killer whales scour the sea in large hunting packs, like wolves, searching for unsuspecting prey. As one of the top members of the ocean's food chain, orca whales are fearless predators, often devouring aquatic creatures as diverse as seals, penguins, and large baleen whales. But what is the typical lifestyle and behavior of an orca whale? Are they as dangerous as legend would have us believe, or are they the docile creatures we see at aquatic theme parks or in movies? The orca whales' true character probably lies somewhere in between these two extremes.

There are numerous myths surrounding orca whales, but few tales come close to reality. Orcas are sea mammals and live in large family groups called pods, which typically contain from 3 to 25 whales. The membership of these pods is stable throughout the lifetime of whales, and it is within these pods that whales communicate, migrate, mate, hunt, and exhibit a myriad of behaviors.

Despite the menacing reputation of the orcas, there have been no known instances in which orca whales have attacked humans. Unfortunately, the reverse is not true. Humans have interfered with the lives of orca whales for centuries, hunting them for meat and blubber or capturing them for use in aquatic parks throughout the world.

1. **Recognizing Words in Context**

   Find the word *scour* in the passage. One definition below is closest to the meaning of that word. One definition has the opposite or nearly opposite meaning. The remaining definition has a completely different meaning. Label the definitions C for *closest,* O for *opposite or nearly opposite,* and D for *different.*

   _____ a. to search out
   _____ b. to depart from
   _____ c. to avoid contact with

2. **Distinguishing Fact from Opinion**

   Two of the statements below present *facts*, which can be proved correct. The other statement is an *opinion,* which expresses someone's thoughts or beliefs. Label the statements F for *fact* and O for *opinion*.

   _____ a. Pods are generally stable throughout the lifetime of a whale.
   _____ b. Pods are better family structures than most species have.
   _____ c. Family units offer species some advantages.

3. **Keeping Events in Order**
   Label the statements below 1, 2, and 3 to show the order in which the events happen.
   _____ a. The orca takes a breath.
   _____ b. An orca whale shoots vapor through its blowhole.
   _____ c. The orca dives deep into the water to chase a seal.

4. **Making Correct Inferences**
   Two of the statements below are correct *inferences*, or reasonable guesses. They are based on information in the passage. The other statement is an incorrect, or faulty, inference. Label the statements C for *correct* inference and F for *faulty* inference.
   _____ a. Orca whales have been misunderstood by people in the past.
   _____ b. There is no way an orca whale could harm a human.
   _____ c. Orca whales display a wide range of behaviors, just as human beings do.

5. **Understanding Main Ideas**
   One of the statements below expresses the main idea of the passage. One statement is too general, or too broad. The other explains only part of the passage; it is too narrow. Label the statements M for *main idea*, B for *too broad*, and N for *too narrow*.
   _____ a. The dolphin family includes killer whales and bottlenose dolphins.
   _____ b. Killer whales live in family units called pods.
   _____ c. Many people have wrong ideas about killer whales.

Correct Answers, Part A _____

Correct Answers, Part B _____

Total Correct Answers _____

3 A What Is a Mineral?

Have you ever played the game Twenty Questions? If so, you may have been asked the question "Is it animal, vegetable, or mineral?" The definition of *mineral* in chemistry, however, differs from the definition of *mineral* in Twenty Questions. What exactly is meant by a mineral in chemistry terms? Minerals share five basic characteristics in chemistry. If a material lacks even one of these characteristics, the material is not a mineral.

To begin with, minerals must be naturally occurring. Scientists define "naturally occurring" as coming from natural processes within the earth. Because minerals come from the earth, they are indeed naturally occurring. For example, many minerals originate from melted rock called magma that comes from deep within Earth. Over time, some of the magma rises to the surface, and large glassy particles called crystals are formed. Crystals come in a variety of colors and include quartz and diamond.

Minerals must also be inorganic. Organic substances are formed from the remains of living creatures and include coal and oil. Inorganic material is devoid of any organic matter.

Additionally, minerals have a solid structure. Unlike gases and liquids that expand to fill whatever container they are placed in, minerals maintain a constant solid shape.

Not only must minerals be solid but they also must have a fixed chemical makeup. Minerals are made from atoms that are linked in specific ways. For example, common salt is always composed of one chlorine (Cl) atom bonded to one sodium (Na) atom. These atoms form one NaCl molecule. Therefore, no matter how much salt, or sodium chloride, is present, it is always arranged in a one-to-one ratio of sodium (Na) to chlorine (Cl) atoms.

The final feature required of minerals is that their individual atoms be organized into regularly repeated patterns. These patterns are called crystal structures. Crystals are similar to a set of blocks, stacked alongside and on top of one another. What distinguishes crystals from other materials is that crystals have a three-dimensional shape that is consistently repeated throughout the substance. For example, a salt crystal has a cubic structure. This means that the atoms that make up salt are arranged in a cube, similar in appearance to a cube of sugar, only much smaller. Therefore, no matter where the salt comes from, the sodium (Na) and chlorine (Cl) atoms tend to arrange themselves naturally into blocks of cube-shaped crystals.

Reading Time _____

Recalling Facts

1. One distinctive feature of a crystal is its
   - a. liquid consistency.
   - b. organic nature.
   - c. three-dimensional shape.

2. An example of a mineral in chemistry is
   - a. a plant.
   - b. coal.
   - c. salt.

3. Materials produced from living organisms or the remains of living organisms are classified as
   - a. organic.
   - b. minerals.
   - c. inorganic.

4. The crystal structure of salt is
   - a. hexagonal.
   - b. cubic.
   - c. tetrahedral.

5. The individual atoms of minerals are organized in regularly repeated patterns called _____ structures.
   - a. solid
   - b. organic
   - c. crystal

Understanding Ideas

6. Many minerals form from magma that rises to the surface and hardens, which means that minerals are
   - a. gaseous.
   - b. solid.
   - c. manufactured.

7. The term "naturally occurring" would probably apply to all of the following *except*
   - a. rocks.
   - b. plastic.
   - c. crystals.

8. A mineral is most likely to originate from
   - a. coal.
   - b. hardened lava.
   - c. fossil remains.

9. You can conclude that
   - a. minerals are extremely rare.
   - b. all minerals are as valuable as diamonds.
   - c. minerals come in a variety of crystal structures.

10. It can be inferred that CaO_2 has
    - a. two calcium (Ca) atoms and one oxygen (O) atom.
    - b. one calcium (Ca) atom and two oxygen (O) atoms.
    - c. one carbon (C) atom and two oxygen (O) atoms.

3 B Moh's Scale of Mineral Hardness

Geologists are always looking for ways to classify unknown minerals. Although there are several methods for determining a mineral's identity, its relative strength is the method most often used. The strength of a mineral is referred to as its hardness. Geologists must do much of their work outdoors, and so they frequently need an expeditious way to determine the hardness of the minerals they encounter. One way to test minerals involves rubbing them against several known materials. They are then checked against a special hardness scale.

Moh's hardness scale is the most common measure used to represent a mineral's hardness. The scale is arranged from 1 to 10. One represents the softest mineral, talc. Ten represents the hardest mineral, diamond. All other naturally occurring minerals have a hardness value somewhere in between.

To determine the hardness of a mineral, geologists first test it against a different material with a known hardness value, such as a fingernail, which has a value of 2.5. If the mineral is easily scratched with a fingernail, its hardness measures less than 2.5. If the mineral is not scratched, the hardness is greater than 2.5, and it must be tested against even harder materials. This process of testing is continued until the mineral is scratched and its hardness, and therefore identity, is determined. If nothing will scratch a mineral, then it must be a diamond, the hardest mineral in nature.

1. **Recognizing Words in Context**

   Find the word *expeditious* in the passage. One definition below is closest to the meaning of that word. One definition has the opposite or nearly opposite meaning. The remaining definition has a completely different meaning. Label the definitions C for *closest*, O for *opposite or nearly opposite*, and D for *different*.

   _____ a. quick and effective
   _____ b. difficult and accurate
   _____ c. slow and useless

2. **Distinguishing Fact from Opinion**

   Two of the statements below present *facts*, which can be proved correct. The other statement is an *opinion*, which expresses someone's thoughts or beliefs. Label the statements F for *fact* and O for *opinion*.

   _____ a. Finding a mineral's hardness value is the best way to identify it.
   _____ b. Moh's hardness scale is arranged from 1 to 10.
   _____ c. If a mineral is scratched by a fingernail, it must have a hardness of less than 2.5.

23

3. **Keeping Events in Order**

   Label the statements below 1, 2, and 3 to show the order in which the events happen.

   _____ a. A mineral is scratched with a material of known hardness.

   _____ b. The mineral is identified.

   _____ c. The mineral is not scratched, and it is tested against harder minerals.

4. **Making Correct Inferences**

   Two of the statements below are correct *inferences,* or reasonable guesses. They are based on information in the passage. The other statement is an incorrect, or faulty, inference. Label the statements C for *correct* inference and F for *faulty* inference.

   _____ a. All minerals that are unidentified must be diamonds.

   _____ b. Geologists often use Moh's hardness scale.

   _____ c. Geologists sometimes attempt to identify minerals outside of a laboratory.

5. **Understanding Main Ideas**

   One of the statements below expresses the main idea of the passage. One statement is too general, or too broad. The other explains only part of the passage; it is too narrow. Label the statements M for *main idea,* B for *too broad,* and N for *too narrow.*

   _____ a. Moh's hardness scale provides a quick and easy way to identify minerals.

   _____ b. Minerals can be identified by their hardness.

   _____ c. Moh's hardness scale gives diamond a value of 10.

Correct Answers, Part A _____

Correct Answers, Part B _____

Total Correct Answers _____

4 A   Global Warming

According to most scientists, the temperature on Earth is expected to increase during the next century. This rise in temperature is known among scientists as global warming. Global warming is defined as an increase in the average temperature of the atmosphere throughout the world. Although this warming trend may seem minor, some experts think it might have lasting effects. One outcome could be a rise in sea levels and the flooding of low-lying areas as a result of the melting of large areas of ice at the North and South Poles. Although other possible outcomes are unclear, global warming appears to be a subject that needs serious attention.

To understand global warming, we must first understand the way our atmosphere is warmed by the Sun. During the day, radiant energy from the Sun warms both Earth's atmosphere and its surface. At night, however, the atmosphere cools down as heat is released from the atmosphere back into space. This process of warming and cooling results in daily temperature changes. When there is more radiant energy in the atmosphere, the temperature is higher.

Earth's atmosphere extends upward from Earth's surface until it forms a border with outer space. The atmosphere is composed of different types of gases, including water vapor and carbon dioxide. Some of these gases are "greenhouse gases." Greenhouse gases differ from other atmospheric gases because they absorb heat but do not release the heat at night. Greenhouse gases get their name because they act like a greenhouse, which keeps plants warm by trapping the Sun's heat within their walls. Similarly, greenhouse gases are like an invisible shield around Earth, keeping some heat from escaping into space.

Although greenhouse gases have always existed, many scientists think the amount of greenhouse gases in our atmosphere is increasing. Specifically, many scientists think the amount of one greenhouse gas, carbon dioxide (CO_2), is rapidly increasing and has risen by 8 percent in the past 25 years.

These scientists speculate that carbon dioxide levels have increased because carbon dioxide is released into the atmosphere when energy-producing substances called fossil fuels are burned. Fossil fuels include petroleum, coal, and natural gas. Fossil fuels come from the remains of animals and are the world's most widely used energy sources.

As energy needs have grown, people throughout the world have increased their fossil fuel consumption. This has increased carbon dioxide levels and may be causing serious global warming.

Reading Time _____

Recalling Facts

1. An increase in the average temperature of the atmosphere throughout the world is known as
   - ❑ a. global warming.
   - ❑ b. the greenhouse effect.
   - ❑ c. the radiation curve.

2. Which of the following is one possible outcome of global warming?
   - ❑ a. deforestation
   - ❑ b. flooding
   - ❑ c. volcanic eruptions

3. Petroleum, coal, and natural gas are classified as
   - ❑ a. biomass fuels.
   - ❑ b. fossil fuels.
   - ❑ c. synthetic fuels.

4. Carbon dioxide is a
   - ❑ a. fossil fuel.
   - ❑ b. greenhouse gas.
   - ❑ c. liquid at room temperature.

5. The amount of the greenhouse gas CO_2 is thought to have increased by _____ percent.
   - ❑ a. 15
   - ❑ b. 22
   - ❑ c. 8

Understanding Ideas

6. According to the article, greenhouse gases keep heat in Earth's atmosphere by
   - ❑ a. not releasing some heat energy at night.
   - ❑ b. destroying the atmosphere's ozone layer.
   - ❑ c. allowing more sunlight into the atmosphere.

7. According to the article, non-greenhouse gases probably have _____ heat energy than greenhouse gases.
   - ❑ a. less
   - ❑ b. more
   - ❑ c. the same

8. If large areas of ice melted, there would be flooding because
   - ❑ a. rivers such as the Mississippi would overflow.
   - ❑ b. ocean levels would rise.
   - ❑ c. dams would burst.

9. If the burning of fossil fuels continues, the amount of carbon dioxide in the atmosphere will likely
   - ❑ a. stay the same.
   - ❑ b. decrease.
   - ❑ c. increase.

10. The burning of fossil fuels has increased in recent years probably because
    - ❑ a. fewer people are using nuclear energy.
    - ❑ b. worldwide populations have increased.
    - ❑ c. other energy sources are increasingly unavailable to people.

4 B Mario J. Molina and the Banning of CFCs

The ozone layer can be thought of as a protective shield surrounding Earth. This layer is very important to humans. It protects living things from the Sun's harmful rays and makes life on Earth possible. Unfortunately, human activity has partially destroyed this lifesaving layer. It was not until the work of Professor Mario J. Molina of the Massachusetts Institute of Technology that we understood how human beings were causing the ozone layer to break apart. Molina explained how chemicals, such as chlorine (Cl) and fluorine (F), were breaking ozone apart in Earth's upper atmosphere.

Molina's work was very important because it led the way for environmental controls on a global level. He accomplished this by being the first to propose that a group of chemicals called chlorofluorocarbons, or CFCs, destroys ozone. His research showed that people needed to stop using CFCs because just one CFC particle can destroy 100,000 ozone particles.

Molina's work also was very important because CFCs were commonly used at the time in a variety of household products, such as hairspray and deodorant. The reaction to Molina's work was phenomenal and led the way for worldwide environmental reform. Following his work, the use of CFC products was banned in many countries. Molina was awarded the 1995 Nobel Prize in chemistry.

1. **Recognizing Words in Context**
   Find the word *phenomenal* in the passage. One definition below is closest to the meaning of that word. One definition has the opposite or nearly opposite meaning. The remaining definition has a completely different meaning. Label the definitions C for *closest,* O for *opposite or nearly opposite,* and D for *different.*
   _____ a. extraordinary
   _____ b. unexceptional
   _____ c. disruptive

2. **Distinguishing Fact from Opinion**
   Two of the statements below present *facts,* which can be proved correct. The other statement is an *opinion,* which expresses someone's thoughts or beliefs. Label the statements F for *fact* and O for *opinion.*
   _____ a. CFC molecules destroy ozone particles.
   _____ b. The ozone layer needs to be protected.
   _____ c. CFC products are banned in many countries.

3. **Keeping Events in Order**

   Label the statements below 1, 2, and 3 to show the order in which the events happen.

   _____ a. CFC molecules destroy ozone in the upper atmosphere.

   _____ b. CFC molecules are released from household products, such as hairspray.

   _____ c. CFC molecules enter the atmosphere.

4. **Making Correct Inferences**

   Two of the statements below are correct *inferences,* or reasonable guesses. They are based on information in the passage. The other statement is an incorrect, or faulty, inference. Label the statements C for *correct* inference and F for *faulty* inference.

   _____ a. CFC molecules are damaging to the ozone layer.

   _____ b. CFC products are available in some countries.

   _____ c. It is impossible to buy a product that uses CFCs.

5. **Understanding Main Ideas**

   One of the statements below expresses the main idea of the passage. One statement is too general, or too broad. The other explains only part of the passage; it is too narrow. Label the statements M for *main idea,* B for *too broad,* and N for *too narrow.*

   _____ a. Molina's research helped explain how CFC molecules harmed the ozone layer.

   _____ b. Molina won the Nobel Prize in chemistry for his work on CFCs.

   _____ c. Large holes have opened up in the ozone layer.

Correct Answers, Part A _____

Correct Answers, Part B _____

Total Correct Answers _____

5 A The Renaissance: A Rebirth of Learning

In about the 14th century, a true revolution began in Europe. This change marked the transition from the Middle Ages to an era called the Renaissance. *Renaissance* is a French word meaning "rebirth." The Renaissance marked a major rebirth of classical learning in Europe. This type of learning was based on the ideas of ancient Greece and Rome. The Renaissance continued through the 15th and 16th centuries.

During the Renaissance, daily life in Europe changed greatly. One of the most important changes resulted from the printing press. In the mid-1400s Johannes Gutenberg perfected a printing press that could mass-produce books. Previously, books had to be copied by hand, one at a time. The printing press made printed materials less expensive and extended book ownership beyond the hands of a privileged few to those of the middle class. As a result, the book industry flourished in Europe, creating both a stronger economy and a better-educated public.

As books became more common, people rediscovered classical literature. Among these works were the writings of such ancient Greek thinkers as Aristotle and Plato. Slowly, the philosophy of these men and other wise men of ancient Greece and Rome began to shape the way that Europeans viewed their world. New concepts about government, science, art, and poetry swept through Europe.

The Renaissance was also a time of exploration and trade. Cartography, the science of mapmaking, became more sophisticated and sparked new interest. Shipbuilding also improved as sailing replaced traditional boating methods that had required the use of many people working the oars. Magnetic compasses and astrolabes enabled explorers to discover new lands. These devices were used to measure latitude by using the Sun and other stars as references. Europeans began trading more with people from distant lands.

One of the most significant trends of the Renaissance was the merging of art, mathematics, and science. Unlike traditional artists, some Renaissance painters began to draw realistic scenes by observation. They did this by studying objects from close up and far away, noting differences in detail and light. This helped them to create beautifully detailed religious paintings.

Using this system of perspective, artists began creating detailed drawings of human anatomy. Leonardo da Vinci applied the principles of science, drawing the human body as an intricate machine integrating structure and function. Such drawings helped spur the scientific revolution to follow and created new directions for virtually every aspect of European life.

Reading Time _____

Recalling Facts

1. The Renaissance occurred from approximately the
   - ❏ a. 14th through 16th centuries.
   - ❏ b. 15th through 17th centuries.
   - ❏ c. 13th through 15th centuries.

2. *Renaissance* is a French word that means
   - ❏ a. new.
   - ❏ b. rebirth.
   - ❏ c. exploration.

3. The Renaissance saw a reemergence of classical literature written by
   - ❏ a. Aristotle and Kant.
   - ❏ b. Aristotle and Plato.
   - ❏ c. Plato and Russell.

4. The printing press was perfected by
   - ❏ a. Aristotle.
   - ❏ b. da Vinci.
   - ❏ c. Gutenberg.

5. The science of mapmaking is called
   - ❏ a. geography.
   - ❏ b. cartography.
   - ❏ c. navigation.

Understanding Ideas

6. It is possible to conclude from the article that people did not read as much prior to the invention of the printing press because they lacked
   - ❏ a. access to books.
   - ❏ b. intelligence.
   - ❏ c. patience.

7. The greatest advantage of sails over the use of oars in ships is probably
   - ❏ a. a reduction in the number of people and supplies needed per voyage.
   - ❏ b. the reliability of wind.
   - ❏ c. the need for less wood.

8. It is possible to conclude from the article that the Renaissance was a time of
   - ❏ a. boredom.
   - ❏ b. excitement.
   - ❏ c. rapid inflation.

9. Artists are most likely to think that the integration of mathematical concepts is
   - ❏ a. too difficult to bother with.
   - ❏ b. not important when creating art.
   - ❏ c. essential for creating realistic images.

10. New navigational technologies such as compasses and astrolabes probably
    - ❏ a. allowed explorers to travel to unknown places.
    - ❏ b. had little effect.
    - ❏ c. confused traditional explorers.

5 B   Leonardo da Vinci

Leonardo da Vinci (1452–1519) was a painter, sculptor, and inventor who lived in Italy during the Renaissance period. This time was unique in Europe because it introduced new ideas in art, literature, science, and culture, including a shift in the way life was reflected through art. Leonardo da Vinci led other painters in creating art based on realistic portrayals of objects and space.

Leonardo used many of the mathematical and scientific concepts developed during the Renaissance to portray how people, animals, and scenery actually looked. Among these newly found ideas were differences in proportionality, distance, and lighting.

Leonardo's artwork reflected differences in distance by showing images scaled to the appropriate dimensions and by correctly reflecting differences in light. Close objects were larger, brighter, and more detailed, while distant objects were smaller, darker, and more obscure. He also used color to add detail and created unique dyes to reflect texture and evoke emotion in his subjects.

Leonardo also created detailed drawings of human anatomy. He was the first artist to illustrate body function through structure. He did this by taking real organs, such as an animal heart, and drawing them through observation. He made arteries look as though blood was actually flowing through them, while the heart, as a whole, appeared to be pumping.

1. **Recognizing Words in Context**

    Find the word *obscure* in the passage. One definition below is closest to the meaning of that word. One definition has the opposite or nearly opposite meaning. The remaining definition has a completely different meaning. Label the definitions C for *closest*, O for *opposite or nearly opposite*, and D for *different*.

    _____ a. unclear

    _____ b. objective

    _____ c. detailed

2. **Distinguishing Fact from Opinion**

    Two of the statements below present *facts*, which can be proved correct. The other statement is an *opinion*, which expresses someone's thoughts or beliefs. Label the statements F for *fact* and O for *opinion*.

    _____ a. Leonardo da Vinci was a famous person.

    _____ b. Leonardo da Vinci created detailed illustrations of the heart.

    _____ c. Leonardo da Vinci integrated math and science to create great art.

3. **Keeping Events in Order**

   Label the statements below 1, 2, and 3 to show the order in which the events happened.

   _____ a. The Renaissance began in Europe.

   _____ b. Modern painters use techniques created by Leonardo da Vinci.

   _____ c. Leonardo da Vinci created artwork based on realistic portrayals of objects and space.

4. **Making Correct Inferences**

   Two of the statements below are correct *inferences,* or reasonable guesses. They are based on information in the passage. The other statement is an incorrect, or faulty, inference. Label the statements C for *correct* inference and F for *faulty* inference.

   _____ a. Most of Leonardo da Vinci's paintings focused on human anatomy.

   _____ b. Leonardo da Vinci was an influential artist.

   _____ c. Prior to the Renaissance, paintings did not show lighting as realistically as many do now.

5. **Understanding Main Ideas**

   One of the statements below expresses the main idea of the passage. One statement is too general, or too broad. The other explains only part of the passage; it is too narrow. Label the statements M for *main idea*, B for *too broad*, and N for *too narrow*.

   _____ a. The Renaissance was an important period in history.

   _____ b. Leonardo da Vinci was a Renaissance painter who created unique artistic techniques.

   _____ c. Leonardo da Vinci created a drawing of an animal heart.

Correct Answers, Part A _____

Correct Answers, Part B _____

Total Correct Answers _____

6 A   What Is a Geneticist?

Inside every cell is the blueprint for life. A complex set of instructions governs the body's many activities and distinguishes one person from another. The wondrous material that directs life is called DNA, which stands for deoxyribonucleic acid. Every living organism, from plants to humans, has DNA inside the nucleus of its cells.

Specific segments of DNA are called genes. They control many processes within an organism. For example, one gene might instruct the body to make a protein needed for digestion. Another gene might control a hormone needed for reproduction. Unfortunately, if the body needs the protein or hormone and the genes are not functioning properly, complications arise.

Genetics is the study of how genes interact to meet an organism's needs. Scientists who work in genetics are called geneticists. There are many fields of genetics. These include genetic disorders and genetic engineering.

Geneticists who study genetic disorders are concerned with certain types of diseases or conditions. These diseases or conditions result from a mutation, or change, in the DNA. Mutations can cause such disorders as Down's syndrome, which is a form of mental retardation, and Huntington's disease, a type of nerve disorder. Geneticists study disorders of this nature because DNA is passed on from generation to generation. If a person's DNA is defective, it may be passed on to the person's children.

Another field of genetics is called genetic engineering. Genetic engineering involves changing DNA to produce a difference in an organism's genes. This is often done with plants. In most cases, geneticists alter the DNA of a plant to help it grow in areas where it might not normally be able to survive. For example, a type of corn may require a certain percentage of nitrogen in the soil in order to grow. In some areas where corn is needed, however, the percentage of nitrogen in the soil may be below the levels necessary for growth. Geneticists might then take the corn and alter a series of genes in the corn's DNA until they find a DNA strand that controls the way the corn responds to nitrogen levels.

Genetically engineered corn, as well as other genetically modified foods, is becoming more widely used, and many people think such foods may help solve food shortage problems. Other people think that genetically altered foods are dangerous because we are uncertain of their long-term effects. Despite such contrasting viewpoints, genetic-engineering research will continue to expand.

Reading Time _____

Recalling Facts

1. The blueprint of life is
   - a. RNA.
   - b. DNA.
   - c. nuclear material.

2. The study of genes is called
   - a. genetics.
   - b. radiology.
   - c. genetic engineering.

3. An example of a genetically based disorder is
   - a. Carpenter's disease.
   - b. tunnel vision.
   - c. Down's syndrome.

4. Genetic engineers have recently learned how to modify
   - a. food.
   - b. automobiles.
   - c. atoms.

5. DNA is located in the
   - a. nucleus.
   - b. central nervous system.
   - c. cerebral cortex.

Understanding Ideas

6. It is possible to conclude from the article that many possible areas of genetic research are
   - a. harmful.
   - b. unexplored.
   - c. unnecessary.

7. The article suggests that genetically altered foods may help alleviate
   - a. the need for fertilizer.
   - b. world hunger.
   - c. genetic disorders.

8. The work of a genetic engineer focuses on
   - a. hormones.
   - b. bacteria.
   - c. DNA.

9. The article suggests that plants can be modified to
   - a. switch from one species to another.
   - b. behave more like animals.
   - c. grow under difficult conditions.

10. From the article, it is possible to conclude that learning more about genes is making genetic disorders
    - a. more common.
    - b. increasingly detectable.
    - c. nonexistent.

6 B   Rosalind Franklin and the Structure of DNA

The structure of DNA was not known until 1953. It was then that two scientists named James Watson and Francis Crick amazed the scientific world by creating an accurate model of the structure of DNA. At the time, scientists all over the world were scrambling to determine DNA's complicated structure. The research was part of a new scientific field called molecular biology. Every biologist knew that whoever correctly identified DNA's structure would be forever famous.

Using data compiled by Rosalind Franklin, Watson and Crick came up with the structure of DNA. Franklin was a researcher at King's College, a part of the University of London. Watson and Crick were able to determine that the shape of a DNA molecule is a double helix, which looks like a ladder twisted into a spiral.

Rosalind Franklin's research involved determining the structure of microscopic objects by creating X-ray diffraction patterns. X-ray diffraction is a technique in which X-rays are beamed at a substance to produce an image. This image shows an outline of the substance's smallest parts and can be used to determine the molecular structure of the substance.

Although researchers had used X-ray diffraction before, Rosalind Franklin was the first to use it to look at DNA. The data from her experiments helped Watson and Crick to discover the long-sought-after structure of DNA.

1. **Recognizing Words in Context**

   Find the word *diffraction* in the passage. One definition below is closest to the meaning of that word. One definition has the opposite or nearly opposite meaning. The remaining definition has a completely different meaning. Label the definitions C for *closest*, O for *opposite or nearly opposite*, and D for *different*.

   _____ a. breaking apart

   _____ b. differentiation

   _____ c. combining

2. **Distinguishing Fact from Opinion**

   Two of the statements below present *facts*, which can be proved correct. The other statement is an *opinion*, which expresses someone's thoughts or beliefs. Label the statements F for *fact* and O for *opinion*.

   _____ a. DNA has a double helix structure.

   _____ b. Franklin would have discovered the structure of DNA if Watson and Crick had not.

   _____ c. Watson and Crick used data from Franklin's research to help them determine the structure of DNA.

35

3. **Keeping Events in Order**

   Label the statements below 1, 2, and 3 to show the order in which the events happened.

   _____ a. Rosalind Franklin created X-ray diffraction patterns of DNA.

   _____ b. Using Franklin's data, Watson and Crick came up with a structure of DNA.

   _____ c. Watson and Crick brought their model of DNA to the scientific community.

4. **Making Correct Inferences**

   Two of the statements below are correct *inferences*, or reasonable guesses. They are based on information in the passage. The other statement is an incorrect, or faulty, inference. Label the statements C for *correct* inference and F for *faulty* inference.

   _____ a. Without the work of Rosalind Franklin, no one would have determined the structure of DNA.

   _____ b. Since 1953, we have learned more about DNA.

   _____ c. Learning the structure of DNA has led to other scientific discoveries.

5. **Understanding Main Ideas**

   One of the statements below expresses the main idea of the passage. One statement is too general, or too broad. The other explains only part of the passage; it is too narrow. Label the statements M for *main idea,* B for *too broad,* and N for *too narrow.*

   _____ a. Rosalind Franklin created X-ray diffraction patterns of DNA.

   _____ b. The development of a model of the DNA molecule was a major scientific breakthrough.

   _____ c. James Watson and Francis Crick correctly identified the structure of DNA using Rosalind Franklin's valuable research.

Correct Answers, Part A _____

Correct Answers, Part B _____

Total Correct Answers _____

7 A The Beauty of Orchids

The orchid is one of the most beautiful and versatile flowers. It can be found growing in many different places, from riverbeds to open meadows, through deep forests, and even on mountainsides. Although many tropical orchids blossom on the branches of trees, others grow on the ground and develop complex root systems. Some orchid species even grow on rocks, using the rocks to anchor their roots.

Orchids have a vibrant history, full of folklore and myth. Ancient Greeks thought orchids had an intoxicating influence over people. Europeans throughout the Middle Ages used orchids for medicinal purposes in a host of herbal remedies. The Chinese thought orchids were a symbol of exalted status and luxury and proclaimed their fragrance to be the fragrance of royalty. Today, people use orchids to decorate their homes, celebrate important events, and beautify their gardens, among other things.

Orchids are not only abundant and alluring but also diverse. There are several hundred orchid species, and they actually make up the world's largest plant family. In fact, there are more than 200 species of orchids in North America alone.

Although orchids are disappearing from the wild as land is cleared for development, many still exist in remote regions. Along the East Coast of the United States, many orchid species flourish as they always have. In several Eastern states, there are literally hundreds of different orchid species growing in the mountains and meadows and along the shorelines.

The flowers of orchids bloom in interesting ways, with some orchids blooming only once in a multiyear cycle. These flowers will bloom one year, only to lie dormant for many years to follow. Other orchids may bloom for only one day per season. Therefore, the variety and behavior of orchids are practically limitless.

Despite their differences, all orchids have the same basic structure—three separate sepals and three petals. Sepals are the leaves around the outside of the flower. The center petal is a structure called the labellum, or lip. This structure serves as the landing platform for insects that pollinate the orchid.

Like all flowers, orchids must be pollinated to ensure new seed formation. Many species of orchids have developed specific blooms attracting only one type of insect to pollinate them. For example, some orchid species are pollinated only by night-flying moths, and so they release more fragrance at night to attract the attention of their pollinator.

Reading Time _____

Recalling Facts

1. Throughout the Middle Ages, Europeans used orchids to make
   - ❏ a. food.
   - ❏ b. tea.
   - ❏ c. medicine.

2. The center orchid petal is called the
   - ❏ a. labellum.
   - ❏ b. sepal.
   - ❏ c. stalk.

3. Like all flowers, orchids are
   - ❏ a. wonderfully fragrant.
   - ❏ b. pollinated.
   - ❏ c. complex.

4. In North America there are more than _____ species of orchids.
   - ❏ a. 200
   - ❏ b. 2,000
   - ❏ c. 100

5. Another word for *labellum* is
   - ❏ a. leaf.
   - ❏ b. petal.
   - ❏ c. lip.

Understanding Ideas

6. According to the article, wild orchids are disappearing from the wild due to
   - ❏ a. global warming.
   - ❏ b. land development.
   - ❏ c. soil changes.

7. The article suggests that orchid pollination is
   - ❏ a. unimportant.
   - ❏ b. complex.
   - ❏ c. necessary.

8. The article suggests that orchids
   - ❏ a. have little variation in bloom cycles.
   - ❏ b. are limited in form.
   - ❏ c. are diverse.

9. Two orchid species with different blooms and fragrances probably have different
   - ❏ a. life cycles.
   - ❏ b. pollinators.
   - ❏ c. nutritional needs.

10. Orchids have probably existed for
    - ❏ a. a short time.
    - ❏ b. a long time.
    - ❏ c. as little as 30 years.

7 B — How to Grow Orchids from Seed

Growing orchids from seed is a long but rewarding process. Although it is true that some species are native to tropical trees and can be difficult to grow, many orchids are terrestrial. Terrestrial orchids grow readily under a variety of conditions. The first step in growing orchids from seed is to choose a species that is compatible with the level of moisture, lighting, and temperature you can provide. Investigate your options in a book about growing orchids.

Water is one of the most critically important factors for successful growth of orchids. If you have a water softener, make sure the water is not softened by salt. Salt will slowly dry the orchid and kill it within six months.

Once you have determined an appropriate orchid species, you will be ready to begin growing your orchid. First, place the seeds into a sterile glass container with a mixture of sugar and nutrients specific for the species chosen. The container will function like a small, self-sufficient greenhouse, maintaining consistent moisture and warmth levels.

The seeds must remain in the container for about a year. Next, purchase potting soil designed for orchids and put it in a flowerpot. Place the seeds into the soil and grow them in the pot for eight months to a year, depending upon the species. Make certain that you follow water, temperature, and lighting guidelines. When the seeds sprout, separate the sprouts into different pots; they will grow for up to seven years before blooming.

1. **Recognizing Words in Context**

   Find the word *terrestrial* in the passage. One definition below is closest to the meaning of that word. One definition has the opposite or nearly opposite meaning. The remaining definition has a completely different meaning. Label the definitions C for *closest*, O for *opposite or nearly opposite*, and D for *different*.

   _____ a. in trees

   _____ b. territorial

   _____ c. on the ground

2. **Distinguishing Fact from Opinion**

   Two of the statements below present *facts*, which can be proved correct. The other statement is an *opinion*, which expresses someone's thoughts or beliefs. Label the statements F for *fact* and O for *opinion*.

   _____ a. Orchids are very difficult to grow.

   _____ b. Orchid seeds must be placed in a sterile flask.

   _____ c. Salt water can kill orchids.

3. **Keeping Events in Order**
   Label the statements below 1, 2, and 3 to show the order in which the events would happen.

   _____ a. Seeds are placed in soil.

   _____ b. Seeds are placed in a sterile flask.

   _____ c. Sprouts are moved into separate pots.

4. **Making Correct Inferences**
   Two of the statements below are correct *inferences*, or reasonable guesses. They are based on information in the passage. The other statement is an incorrect, or faulty, inference. Label the statements C for *correct* inference and F for *faulty* inference.

   _____ a. Some orchids take years to grow.

   _____ b. Nothing but salt water will kill an orchid.

   _____ c. Some orchid species take seven years to bloom.

5. **Understanding Main Ideas**
   One of the statements below expresses the main idea of the passage. One statement is too general, or too broad. The other explains only part of the passage; it is too narrow. Label the statements M for *main idea*, B for *too broad*, and N for *too narrow*.

   _____ a. Orchids can be grown at home.

   _____ b. Orchid seeds must remain in a glass flask for about a year.

   _____ c. Growing orchids from seeds requires patience and attention to detail.

Correct Answers, Part A _____

Correct Answers, Part B _____

Total Correct Answers _____

8 A   The Science of Golf

The principles of science apply to almost every sport imaginable. In golf, for example, the talent of the players often corresponds to how effectively they apply the basic laws of physics. The ultimate goal of golf is to get the golf ball into the hole with as few strokes as possible. Successful golf strategies vary according to the type of golf hole being played. All of these strategies, however, depend on a fundamentally sound golf swing. A good golf swing requires the golfer to be very precise with body movements.

When a golf club strikes a golf ball, force propels the ball forward and upward. This accelerates the ball to approximately the same velocity as that of the club head. The club head is the part of the golf club that makes contact with the ball. In addition to propelling the ball forward, the club head also gives a particular spin to the ball. A good swing creates a spin that helps to lift the ball upward and to keep it in flight longer. This makes for greater distance. The club face, the flat part of the club head, is what actually strikes the ball and gives it spin.

Understanding and applying fundamental laws of physics can help golfers improve their games. First of all, golfers must swing so that the club face is perpendicular to the target when it strikes the ball. This requires correct positioning of many body parts—especially arms, shoulders, hips, and legs—throughout the swing. If the club face is not perpendicular to the target, the ball will have a sideways spin and it will not go straight.

The arc of the swing itself will determine the resultant speed of the ball. This arc is created when the golfer first swings the club backward to the shoulders and then brings the club forward through impact. Proper timing is one of the keys to creating a correct arc.

Finally, a golfer needs to swing with a proper follow-through. The follow-through is the part of the swing that takes place after the ball is hit. To achieve the appropriate follow-through, a golfer must completely extend the arms after the ball has been hit. The golfer should not try to slow down the swing at the end, in the hope of having more control. Slowing down the swing will actually result in less control and a poor shot.

Reading Time _____

Recalling Facts

1. Hitting a golf ball with a club propels the ball
   - a. forward and downward.
   - b. forward and upward.
   - c. backward and straight.

2. A golf swing utilizes the basic laws of
   - a. botany.
   - b. physics.
   - c. engineering.

3. A proper golf swing has
   - a. an ascending angle of approach.
   - b. a proper follow-through.
   - c. a sideways spin.

4. The velocity of a golf ball matches the velocity of the
   - a. arms.
   - b. wind.
   - c. club head.

5. The final part of a golf swing is called
   - a. follow-through.
   - b. the last step.
   - c. the conversion.

Understanding Ideas

6. According to the article, the club face must be _____ to the target.
   - a. concentric
   - b. at right angles
   - c. parallel

7. The article suggests that golf is simply a matter of
   - a. practice.
   - b. understanding and applying the laws of physics.
   - c. a well-designed course.

8. A ball that is spinning to the right will probably travel
   - a. to the right.
   - b. to the left.
   - c. straight.

9. According to the article, extending the arms during the follow-through makes the ball
   - a. arc effectively.
   - b. travel farther and straighter.
   - c. curve to the right.

10. Golf balls eventually come back to the ground because of
    - a. spin.
    - b. gravity.
    - c. bad physics.

8 B The Evolution of the Golf Ball

The game of golf originated in Scotland centuries ago. In those early times, players often created their own handcrafted clubs and balls out of wood. Therefore the quality of the equipment varied with the skill of the player. After competitive play began in the 1500s, however, golfers began to buy equipment made by professional craftspeople, and the equipment became more standardized.

The first official ball, called the featherie, was introduced in 1618. This ball was a collection of goose feathers wrapped in animal hide. As the ball dried, the feathers expanded and the leather shrank to create a tight, hard surface. Although these balls were quite effective and could reach high velocities when hit, the method used to create them typically made balls more expensive than clubs.

The first mass-produced golf ball, called the gutta-percha, was created in 1848. This ball was made by taking sap from a gutta tree and molding it into a spherical shape. Unfortunately, gutta-percha balls had smooth surfaces that tended to create air drag. This limited the distance they could travel.

It was soon discovered that small dents in the surface of golf balls increased their aerodynamic efficiency and allowed them to travel an average of 18 meters (20 yards) farther. This fact led to the creation of the common "dimple" pattern in 1905. The dimple-patterned golf ball, which minimizes air resistance while maximizing lift, has become the standard ball used today.

1. **Recognizing Words in Context**

   Find the word *standardized* in the passage. One definition below is closest to the meaning of that word. One definition has the opposite or nearly opposite meaning. The remaining definition has a completely different meaning. Label the definitions C for *closest*, O for *opposite or nearly opposite*, and D for *different*.

   _____ a. identical

   _____ b. measured

   _____ c. varying

2. **Distinguishing Fact from Opinion**

   Two of the statements below present *facts*, which can be proved correct. The other statement is an *opinion*, which expresses someone's thoughts or beliefs. Label the statements F for *fact* and O for *opinion*.

   _____ a. The featherie was replaced by the gutta-percha ball.

   _____ b. The dimple-patterned golf ball is the standard ball used today.

   _____ c. The featherie was more enjoyable to use than the gutta-percha was.

3. **Keeping Events in Order**

   Label the statements below 1, 2, and 3 to show the order in which the events happened.

   _____ a. The gutta-percha ball was created by molding gutta tree sap.

   _____ b. The dimple-patterned golf ball became the standard golf ball.

   _____ c. The featherie ball was introduced.

4. **Making Correct Inferences**

   Two of the statements below are correct *inferences,* or reasonable guesses. They are based on information in the passage. The other statement is an incorrect, or faulty, inference. Label the statements C for *correct* inference and F for *faulty* inference.

   _____ a. The best golf ball is the one that minimizes air resistance.

   _____ b. The only reason the featherie was replaced was because of its high cost.

   _____ c. Modern golf balls are improved versions of earlier ones.

5. **Understanding Main Ideas**

   One of the statements below expresses the main idea of the passage. One statement is too general, or too broad. The other explains only part of the passage; it is too narrow. Label the statements M for *main idea,* B for *too broad,* and N for *too narrow.*

   _____ a. Golfers play better when they have good equipment.

   _____ b. The featherie was covered with animal hide.

   _____ c. The golf ball has changed over the years.

Correct Answers, Part A _____

Correct Answers, Part B _____

Total Correct Answers _____

9 A — Animal Classification: Vertebrates and Invertebrates

Animals exist in many different forms and in many different locations. There are well over one million animal species, including *Homo sapiens,* a species that consists of human beings. Scientists use classification systems to distinguish one species, or group of species, from another. Some systems classify animals in terms of a specific physical characteristic. Other systems separate species in terms of what they eat or the way in which they grow to adulthood. One of the most common methods for separating species involves classifying them as vertebrates or invertebrates.

Vertebrates are animals with backbones. Vertebrates make up only 5 percent of all animals. Included in this group are birds, fish, and mammals. Some vertebrates have backbones their entire lives. Others have a backbone only as adults. These animals are born with a notochord, a long flexible rod that supports their backs. The animals develop a more rigid skeletal framework as they grow into adults.

Other vertebrates have a backbone throughout their development. In most cases, these vertebrates have a column of multisegmented bones, called vertebrae. The vertebrae are attached to a well-developed brain that processes sensory information. In fact, a highly specialized brain is a basic difference between vertebrates and invertebrates. A vertebrate also has an assortment of sensory organs, such as a nose and eyes.

Vertebrates may communicate with one another in interesting ways. While biologists once thought that only humans communicated, they now believe that other vertebrates communicate as well. For example, mammals as diverse as bats and whales use echolocation—the projection of sound waves—to locate food, and many scientists think they may also use it to communicate with members of their own species.

Invertebrates, which have no backbone, comprise about 95 percent of all animals. This group includes jellyfish, worms, squid, crabs, and insects. Invertebrates are notable for their diversity. Insects alone comprise almost one million species, more than a fourth of which are beetles.

One special feature of insects is the existence of a larval stage during youth. Many insects undergo incomplete metamorphosis, a period during which the larvae, or young, look like adults but are smaller in size. In complete metamorphosis, young larvae look very different from adults. For example, butterflies undergo complete metamorphosis and begin life in a larval stage as a caterpillar. Soon after, the larva encases itself in a cocoon, and finally a beautiful adult butterfly emerges.

Reading Time _____

Recalling Facts

1. Animals with backbones are called
   - a. vertebrates.
   - b. invertebrates.
   - c. larvae.

2. The species name for human beings is
   - a. *Coryphaena hipparus.*
   - b. *Homo sapiens.*
   - c. *Euglena gracilis.*

3. The vertebrate brain is attached to the
   - a. vertebrae.
   - b. heart.
   - c. liver.

4. The number of insect species is approximately
   - a. 100,000.
   - b. 1,000,000.
   - c. 2,000,000.

5. Of all animal species, vertebrates make up only
   - a. 20 percent.
   - b. 10 percent.
   - c. 5 percent.

Understanding Ideas

6. Sensory organs would include all of the following *except*
   - a. feet.
   - b. a nose.
   - c. eyes.

7. An animal chosen at random is most likely to be
   - a. anaerobic.
   - b. a vertebrate.
   - c. an invertebrate.

8. You can conclude from the article that animals that undergo complete metamorphosis are all
   - a. vertebrates.
   - b. invertebrates.
   - c. diverse.

9. Many scientists think echolocation could be used for
   - a. transportation.
   - b. development.
   - c. communication.

10. Complete and incomplete metamorphosis are part of a system used to _____ insects.
    - a. eliminate
    - b. classify
    - c. locate

9 B Cephalopods

Cephalopods are a group of invertebrates that live in the ocean. This group has many species, including the squid, the octopus, and the chambered nautilus.

The word *cephalopod* means "head foot." The reason for this name is that a cephalopod's mouth is actually at the center of its foot, which itself is elongated into several tentacles. Unlike many other species, cephalopods are built for speed. They are carnivores, or meat eaters, and must move quickly to catch prey. Many have mouths with beaklike jaws to catch and crush prey.

Squid are cephalopods. They move very quickly, and usually backwards, by drawing water into their inner cavity and then spraying it out a narrow, jetlike tube at the opposite end. Scientists think that a squid steers by pointing this tube in different directions. Although most squid are small, the giant squid is the largest invertebrate in existence and can reach lengths of 17 meters (56 feet) and weigh as much as 2 tons.

The chambered nautilus is a snail-like creature that is related to a group of shelled cephalopods called ammonites. Ammonites were the dominant predators of the oceans millions of years ago. Like dinosaurs, they became extinct, but the chambered nautilus has survived.

1. **Recognizing Words in Context**

   Find the word *elongated* in the passage. One definition below is closest to the meaning of that word. One definition has the opposite or nearly opposite meaning. The remaining definition has a completely different meaning. Label the definitions C for *closest,* O for *opposite or nearly opposite,* and D for *different.*

   _____ a. extended

   _____ b. shortened

   _____ c. relieved

2. **Distinguishing Fact from Opinion**

   Two of the statements below present *facts,* which can be proved correct. The other statement is an *opinion,* which expresses someone's thoughts or beliefs. Label the statements F for *fact* and O for *opinion.*

   _____ a. The squid is a fascinating cephalopod.

   _____ b. The word *cephalopod* means "head foot."

   _____ c. Some cephalopods have powerful jaws that crush prey.

3. **Keeping Events in Order**

   Label the statements below 1, 2, and 3 to show the order in which the events happen.

   _____ a. A squid draws water into its inner cavity.

   _____ b. A squid captures a shrimp.

   _____ c. A squid squirts water out of its narrow jetlike tube.

4. **Making Correct Inferences**

   Two of the statements below are correct *inferences*, or reasonable guesses. They are based on information in the passage. The other statement is an incorrect, or faulty, inference. Label the statements C for *correct* inference and F for *faulty* inference.

   _____ a. Cephalopods are the fastest predators in the ocean.

   _____ b. Ammonites lacked backbones.

   _____ c. Cephalopods are effective hunters.

5. **Understanding Main Ideas**

   One of the statements below expresses the main idea of the passage. One statement is too general, or too broad. The other explains only part of the passage; it is too narrow. Label the statements M for *main idea*, B for *too broad*, and N for *too narrow*.

   _____ a. Cephalopods are invertebrates that live in the ocean and have tentacles.

   _____ b. The giant squid is the largest invertebrate.

   _____ c. Some invertebrates live in the ocean.

Correct Answers, Part A _____

Correct Answers, Part B _____

Total Correct Answers _____

10 A The Life Cycle of a Star

Stars have life cycles, just as human beings do. Stars are born under certain conditions, live for a period of time, and eventually die. The life span of a star differs from that of a human, however—by billions of years!

Modern telescopes have helped astronomers to learn more about stars. Stars can be compared to huge nuclear reactors creating energy in the form of heat and light. They are the source of all energy within the universe; without stars life would not exist.

Scientists are not sure of the exact process by which a star forms. They believe that the life of a star begins with a gigantic cloud of dust and gas called a nebula. Over time, gravitational forces develop within the cloud, and hydrogen atoms are pulled in toward the center where they fuse into helium atoms, releasing heat and energy. When the temperature of the nebula reaches a critical level, a new star is formed.

Throughout their lifetimes, stars change in both color and temperature. These two characteristics are related. The hottest stars are blue and have a surface temperature of approximately 35,000 °C (63,000 °F). Other stars vary from white to yellow to red-orange to red, and they range in temperature from 10,000 to 3,000 °C. (18,000 to 5,000 °F). As stars get older, they lose energy, their temperatures decrease, and eventually they turn red.

Along with color and temperature, size differs among stars. Our own star, the Sun, is a medium-sized star. Although medium-sized stars live for approximately 10 billion years before they finally lose their energy and cease existence, smaller stars can live up to 100 billion years. Very large stars—known as super-massive stars—live for "only" a few billion years.

A star that is five or more times as massive as the Sun dies when the gravitational collapse of its core triggers a massive explosion called a supernova. Medium-sized stars simply cool down and then slowly perish, becoming dense iron lumps of matter that astronomers call black dwarfs.

Super-massive stars, however, have an entirely different fate. After such a star undergoes a supernova explosion, the core becomes so heavy that it finally collapses under its own gravity, creating a black hole. The gravity of a black hole is so tremendous that it acts like a huge vacuum cleaner in space, pulling in everything in its vicinity.

Reading Time _____

Recalling Facts

1. Stars can be compared to
   - ❏ a. Jupiter.
   - ❏ b. huge nuclear reactors.
   - ❏ c. light bulbs.

2. Scientists believe that a star is formed from a
   - ❏ a. nebula.
   - ❏ b. black dwarf.
   - ❏ c. black hole.

3. The hottest stars are
   - ❏ a. red.
   - ❏ b. blue.
   - ❏ c. yellow.

4. Medium-sized stars live for approximately
   - ❏ a. 10 billion years.
   - ❏ b. 1 million years.
   - ❏ c. 1 billion years.

5. A super-massive star eventually becomes a
   - ❏ a. black dwarf.
   - ❏ b. white dwarf.
   - ❏ c. black hole.

Understanding Ideas

6. It can be inferred that a nebula has
   - ❏ a. a lower temperature than a star.
   - ❏ b. a higher temperature than a star.
   - ❏ c. the same temperatures as a star.

7. Our Sun probably has a temperature of
   - ❏ a. between 10,000 and 3,000 °C.
   - ❏ b. greater than 10,000 °C.
   - ❏ c. approximately 35,000 °C.

8. It is possible to conclude from the article that the larger the mass of a star, the _____ its life span
   - ❏ a. longer
   - ❏ b. shorter
   - ❏ c. simpler

9. What might a black dwarf consist of?
   - ❏ a. fiery gases and exploding atoms
   - ❏ b. a cloud of extremely hot dust
   - ❏ c. a solid mass of iron

10. Our Sun will eventually become a
    - ❏ a. black hole.
    - ❏ b. black dwarf.
    - ❏ c. blue star.

10 B   The Andromeda Galaxy

If you look up in the sky on a clear night, you may see a fuzzy patch of light. This object could well be the Andromeda Galaxy, which is the most distant object visible to the naked eye. It lies more than 2 million light years from Earth. Andromeda is the largest member of the Local Group, a group of 30 galaxies that includes our own Milky Way.

Like the Milky Way, Andromeda is a spiral galaxy. It contains roughly twice the number of stars as the Milky Way, measures 125,000 light years across, and has two cores. Scientists speculate that Andromeda's two cores are the result of a collision of two separate galaxies billions of years ago.

Another unique feature of this galaxy is its emission of tremendous amounts of X-ray light. In outer space, X-ray light usually radiates from objects with extremely high temperatures. This suggests that most of the material within Andromeda is plasma. Plasma is formed when a gas gets so hot that its atoms separate into positive and negative ions. Scientists believe that most of the matter in the universe is in the form of plasma.

Andromeda is interesting because plasma is thought to have been the first material formed in the universe. Therefore, studying Andromeda may provide insight into how our universe began.

1. **Recognizing Words in Context**

   Find the word *emission* in the passage. One definition below is closest to the meaning of that word. One definition has the opposite or nearly opposite meaning. The remaining definition has a completely different meaning. Label the definitions C for *closest*, O for *opposite or nearly opposite*, and D for *different*.

   _____ a. burning up
   _____ b. sending out
   _____ c. bringing in

2. **Distinguishing Fact from Opinion**

   Two of the statements below present *facts*, which can be proved correct. The other statement is an *opinion*, which expresses someone's thoughts or beliefs. Label the statements F for *fact* and O for *opinion*.

   _____ a. The Andromeda Galaxy has roughly twice as many stars as the Milky Way.
   _____ b. The Andromeda Galaxy is one of the most spectacular objects in space.
   _____ c. Plasma emits X-ray light.

3. **Keeping Events in Order**

   Label the statements below 1, 2, and 3 to show the order in which the events happened.

   _____ a. A galaxy with two cores was created.

   _____ b. Two galaxies collided.

   _____ c. A galaxy raced toward another galaxy.

4. **Making Correct Inferences**

   Two of the statements below are correct *inferences*, or reasonable guesses. They are based on information in the passage. The other statement is an incorrect, or faulty, inference. Label the statements C for *correct* inference and F for *faulty* inference.

   _____ a. Most objects in outer space that have low temperatures do not give off much X-ray light.

   _____ b. In terms of galaxies, Andromeda is much older than the Milky Way.

   _____ c. Some galaxies collide with other galaxies.

5. **Understanding Main Ideas**

   One of the statements below expresses the main idea of the passage. One statement is too general, or too broad. The other explains only part of the passage; it is too narrow. Label the statements M for *main idea*, B for *too broad*, and N for *too narrow*.

   _____ a. One type of galaxy is a spiral galaxy.

   _____ b. The Andromeda Galaxy has several important features.

   _____ c. The Andromeda Galaxy contains plasma.

Correct Answers, Part A _____

Correct Answers, Part B _____

Total Correct Answers _____

11 A   Earth's Changing Landscape

Have you ever glanced at a mountain and wondered how it was created? Does it seem incredible that the Grand Canyon was created by water from the Colorado River dissolving rock for millions of years? People wonder about natural formations because they have trouble envisioning Earth's being different from the way it is now.

In reality, Earth is quite dynamic, constantly evolving and changing shape. The difficulty in picturing this transformation stems from the processes being so slow. Many changes take millions of years; people do not witness much change in their lifetimes. Instead, they collect evidence from the past and, like detectives, piece together the clues to decipher Earth's history.

Earth's lithosphere, or rocky outer layer, is constantly changing. This change results from various forces deep within Earth. Earth's interior is brimming with activity as heat is transferred upward. This heat transfer ultimately influences the appearance of the surface.

The lithosphere is fragmented into a number of segments, or plates, that float above a semifluid molten layer of rock called the asthenosphere. As the material within the asthenosphere rises toward Earth's surface, it pushes the lithospheric plates in various directions. As a result, the plates move like bumper cars, crashing and bouncing due to Earth's internal forces. This movement changes the shape of Earth's surface, also called the crust.

Movement of the lithospheric plates can be gradual or sudden. Mountains and volcanoes are formed when two lithospheric plates come together. If this process occurs within a continent, the crust folds, creating mountains. If the plates continue to push together, they can form huge mountain ranges, such as the Alps. When two plates of widely varying weights come together, however, something very different happens. In this case, the heavier lithospheric plate plunges underneath the lighter plate. The pressure becomes so intense that large cracks develop. This allows the molten rock to rise and form volcanoes. The Cascade Range, extending along the Pacific coast, consists of volcanoes that resulted from this process.

Given these dynamic processes, we can see that Earth's landscape is enormously complex and constantly evolving. Its surface is littered with formations that shift in response to the fiery forces deep within Earth's interior. Some of the most dramatic changes occur out of our view, underneath the ocean floor. Over time, dynamic forces create a planet that is rife with diversity and mystery.

Reading Time _____

Recalling Facts

1. Earth's outer rocky layer is known as the
   - ❑ a. lithosphere.
   - ❑ b. mantle.
   - ❑ c. asthenosphere.

2. Lithospheric plates move in response to
   - ❑ a. earthquakes.
   - ❑ b. molten rock rising.
   - ❑ c. gravity.

3. The semifluid molten layer of rock below the lithosphere is called the
   - ❑ a. inner core.
   - ❑ b. asthenosphere.
   - ❑ c. crust.

4. Lithospheric plates move
   - ❑ a. in various directions.
   - ❑ b. in one direction only.
   - ❑ c. so slowly it does not matter.

5. When two plates of widely different weights collide, the heavier plate
   - ❑ a. rises above the lighter one.
   - ❑ b. crashes into the lighter one.
   - ❑ c. plunges underneath the lighter one.

Understanding Ideas

6. According to the article, humans have a hard time conceptualizing events that they
   - ❑ a. think are impossible.
   - ❑ b. doubt have occurred.
   - ❑ c. do not witness themselves.

7. The Rocky Mountains probably resulted from
   - ❑ a. lava flows.
   - ❑ b. two lithospheric plates coming together.
   - ❑ c. an earthquake.

8. The article suggests that lithospheric plates exist
   - ❑ a. all over the world.
   - ❑ b. only in certain areas.
   - ❑ c. exclusively in the United States.

9. It can be inferred that hot materials tend to
   - ❑ a. remain in a fixed location.
   - ❑ b. rise.
   - ❑ c. sink.

10. The surface of Earth will most likely
    - ❑ a. continue to change.
    - ❑ b. remain the same.
    - ❑ c. undergo rapid transformation.

11 B Trees: Anchors of Earth's Crust

Trees play an important role in our lives and furnish a variety of comforts and pleasures. One of the most important aspects of trees is the beauty they bring to nature and to our surroundings. From the bright colors of their leaves in the fall, to their emerging blossoms in the spring, to their abundant supply of fruit in the summer, trees are a continual source of inspiration and nourishment.

Trees also serve a number of practical purposes. For example, they act as an important soil stabilizer. With their deep roots, they provide a home for beneficial fungi that improve the soil and help crops to flourish. Without trees, valuable topsoil would be eroded by rain and wind, making it difficult to cultivate crops on a consistent basis. Trees themselves also provide food, yielding fruit, leaves, and roots to various animal species. The leaves of trees remove carbon dioxide from the air and emit oxygen.

Additionally, trees are an invaluable natural resource, supplying us with wood products. Wood provides numerous necessities of life, such as fuel for fires and structural framework for homes. Wood is also used in the production of a variety of domestic items such as furniture, musical instruments, baseball bats, toothpicks, and even paper. In terms of nonwood products, trees generate items as diverse as tannin for treating leather, pharmaceuticals, maple syrup, fibers, and dyes.

1. **Recognizing Words in Context**

   Find the word *emit* in the passage. One definition below is closest to the meaning of that word. One definition has the opposite or nearly opposite meaning. The remaining definition has a completely different meaning. Label the definitions C for *closest*, O for *opposite or nearly opposite*, and D for *different*.

   _____ a. permit

   _____ b. take in

   _____ c. give off

2. **Distinguishing Fact from Opinion**

   Two of the statements below present *facts*, which can be proved correct. The other statement is an *opinion*, which expresses someone's thoughts or beliefs. Label the statements F for *fact* and O for *opinion*.

   _____ a. Fall is a beautiful time of year.

   _____ b. Trees provide fruit.

   _____ c. Trees enrich the soil.

3. **Keeping Events in Order**

   Label the statements below 1, 2, and 3 to show the order in which the events happen.

   _____ a. Rain washes soil off the hill and creates a mudslide.

   _____ b. Homes are destroyed.

   _____ c. All of the trees on a hillside are cut down.

4. **Making Correct Inferences**

   Two of the statements below are correct *inferences*, or reasonable guesses. They are based on information in the passage. The other statement is an incorrect, or faulty, inference. Label the statements C for *correct* inference and F for *faulty* inference.

   _____ a. Without trees, we would not have as many natural resources as we do now.

   _____ b. We would lead duller lives without trees.

   _____ c. Trees provide food.

5. **Understanding Main Ideas**

   One of the statements below expresses the main idea of the passage. One statement is too general, or too broad. The other explains only part of the passage; it is too narrow. Label the statements M for *main idea*, B for *too broad*, and N for *too narrow*.

   _____ a. Trees benefit our lives in a number of ways.

   _____ b. Trees help to stabilize the soil.

   _____ c. Trees are a common type of plant.

Correct Answers, Part A _____

Correct Answers, Part B _____

Total Correct Answers _____

12 A — How to Avoid Avalanches

Mountains are some of the most impressive formations on Earth. But they can also be some of the most deadly, luring ill-prepared people to their slopes. With little warning, snow-covered mountains can suddenly become unstable, hurling massive amounts of snow rapidly downward. Avalanches claim more than 150 lives per year. Despite the danger, mountain climbers and hikers often do not take the necessary precautions. By understanding the factors that contribute to avalanches, people can minimize their risks and still enjoy the beauty of a snow-capped peak.

Avalanches are usually triggered by some type of vibration. Common causes of such vibrations are strong winds, loud noises, earth tremors, and even the motion of a skier.

Although an avalanche is difficult to predict, there are several elements that increase the chance of its occurring. The first factor to consider is the slope of a mountain. The steeper the mountain, the greater the likelihood of an avalanche. Heavy accumulations of snow tend to weaken more easily on steep mountains, sometimes unleashing an avalanche from only a small vibration. Even though avalanches are possible on almost any slope, most occur on slopes with an angle of more than 30 degrees.

The moisture content of the snow is another key factor in predicting the likelihood of an avalanche. If the mountain slope faces the sun and the snow begins to melt, an avalanche may occur on a slope with an angle as small as 10 degrees. But if the snow is dry and humidity is low, a slope in the sun may be safe to an angle of 25 degrees. Regardless of conditions, slopes of more than 35 degrees should always be avoided.

Another major avalanche risk factor is depth of the snowpack. A snowpack is defined as the total combined mass of snow layered on a mountainside. Avalanches are more likely with deep snowpacks than they are with shallow snowpacks.

As far as weather is concerned, one of the most important things to keep in mind when evaluating risk is to remember that snowpacks are increasingly unstable in changing weather conditions. For example, a light snowfall immediately followed by a heavy snowfall may create an internally weak layer along a slope, making an avalanche more likely. Another risk factor is changing moisture content. A dry snowfall alone is not that dangerous. If it is followed by a wet snowfall, however, the chance of an avalanche increases dramatically.

Reading Time _____

Recalling Facts

1. The number of people killed by avalanches each year is approximately
   - ❏ a. 500.
   - ❏ b. 1,000.
   - ❏ c. 150.

2. As the slope of a mountain increases, the likelihood of an avalanche
   - ❏ a. increases.
   - ❏ b. decreases.
   - ❏ c. stays the same.

3. A light snowfall followed by a heavy snowfall may create
   - ❏ a. a heavy rainfall.
   - ❏ b. an internally weak layer.
   - ❏ c. a trigger.

4. The total collective mass of snow along a mountainside is called a
   - ❏ a. snowpack.
   - ❏ b. snowmass.
   - ❏ c. snowdrift.

5. An example of a trigger is
   - ❏ a. hibernating animals.
   - ❏ b. steep slopes.
   - ❏ c. wind.

Understanding Ideas

6. It would be difficult to determine the stability of a snowpack because
   - ❏ a. the weather often changes several times in an hour.
   - ❏ b. it is hard to see how deep the snowpack is.
   - ❏ c. the stability depends on how many people are hiking.

7. The best approach to take is to always consider mountainsides to be
   - ❏ a. potentially dangerous.
   - ❏ b. deadly.
   - ❏ c. safe.

8. Changing weather conditions can trigger an avalanche because the snow can become
   - ❏ a. hardened.
   - ❏ b. internally unstable.
   - ❏ c. dry and brittle.

9. According to the article, avalanches cannot be predicted with absolute certainty because
   - ❏ a. avalanches are so rare they are seldom studied.
   - ❏ b. many factors create the conditions for an avalanche.
   - ❏ c. no one knows what may trigger an avalanche.

10. People should probably avoid hiking on a snow-packed mountain following a heavy snowfall because
    - ❏ a. the snow is always loose and dry.
    - ❏ b. another heavy snowfall usually follows.
    - ❏ c. the snowpack may be unstable.

12 B Surviving an Avalanche

While hiking up a mountain in winter, you suddenly hear a rumble. You look up and see a pile of snow billowing down toward you at high speed. You don't have time to get out of the way. What should you do? There are a few things you can do that will enhance your chances of survival.

First, yell to anyone who is with you, warning them of the danger and alerting them to your location. Next, drop whatever you are carrying and thrust upward in a swimming-like motion, staying as close to the surface as possible. Finally, try to keep at least one hand above the cascading snow in case you need to dig yourself out after the avalanche has stopped. If you can keep one hand in contact with the air, it will help you to avoid losing your sense of direction if you get buried. If you do get buried and are not able to keep your hand above the surface, spitting can help you figure out which direction you are facing. Gravity will pull your spit in the opposite direction of the surface.

Taking appropriate precautions is the best defense when attempting to avoid avalanches. Hiking on a snow-packed mountain should never be tried within 24 hours of a heavy snowfall or in changing weather conditions. In addition, people should always carry an avalanche beacon and travel in teams.

1. **Recognizing Words in Context**

   Find the word *enhance* in the passage. One definition below is closest to the meaning of that word. One definition has the opposite or nearly opposite meaning. The remaining definition has a completely different meaning. Label the definitions C for *closest*, O for *opposite or nearly opposite*, and D for *different*.

   _____ a. harm
   _____ b. improve
   _____ c. affect

2. **Distinguishing Fact from Opinion**

   Two of the statements below present *facts*, which can be proved correct. The other statement is an *opinion*, which expresses someone's thoughts or beliefs. Label the statements F for *fact* and O for *opinion*.

   _____ a. Avalanches are among the world's most deadly natural disasters.
   _____ b. Avalanches can strike with little warning.
   _____ c. People can do several things to decrease their risk of being in an avalanche.

3. **Keeping Events in Order**

   Label the statements below 1, 2, and 3 to show the order in which the events happen.

   _____ a. Snow along a mountainside suddenly becomes unstable.

   _____ b. Snow begins cascading down a mountain.

   _____ c. Rescue workers look for survivors of the avalanche.

4. **Making Correct Inferences**

   Two of the statements below are correct *inferences*, or reasonable guesses. They are based on information in the passage. The other statement is an incorrect, or faulty, inference. Label the statements C for *correct* inference and F for *faulty* inference.

   _____ a. The more information people have about a mountain, the better their chances for avoiding an avalanche.

   _____ b. Even people who frequently hike in snowy areas can always avoid avalanches by gathering enough information.

   _____ c. Avalanches will always occur.

5. **Understanding Main Ideas**

   One of the statements below expresses the main idea of the passage. One statement is too general, or too broad. The other explains only part of the passage; it is too narrow. Label the statements M for *main idea*, B for *too broad*, and N for *too narrow*.

   _____ a. Avalanches can be dangerous.

   _____ b. Learning about avalanches is the best defense in avoiding or surviving an avalanche.

   _____ c. Do not hike within 24 hours of a heavy snowfall.

Correct Answers, Part A _____

Correct Answers, Part B _____

Total Correct Answers _____

13 A   The Three Phases of Matter

Matter is defined as any object that occupies space and has mass. Matter exists in one of three forms: solid, liquid, or gas. These three forms are referred to as the three phases of matter. Each phase can be converted from one form to another under certain conditions.

Matter can be converted from one phase to another by manipulating the temperature of the material. When pressure remains constant, each type of matter has a characteristic temperature at which a solid will change into a liquid or a liquid will change into a gas. These temperatures are called the melting point and the boiling point, respectively.

A solid is a material with both a definite shape and a definite volume, meaning that a solid will always exist in the same form as long as the temperature remains constant. However, as the temperature increases, the solid will experience a phase change and melt into a liquid. All solid materials have a critical temperature at which they are converted to liquids. This melting point differs according to the type of solid. For example, water is liquid at room temperature (22° C or 72° F) and has a freezing point of 0° C (32° F), yet iron is a solid at room temperature and will not melt until it reaches its melting point of 1100° C (2012° F).

A liquid differs from a solid because a liquid has a definite volume but an indefinite shape. An indefinite shape means that a liquid takes the shape of its container. For example, a liquid can be poured into a tall, thin, 1-liter container or a short, wide, 1-liter container, but both containers will have the same definite volume, or total space.

To contrast the shape of a liquid with the shape of a solid, consider water. While water takes the shape of whatever container it is poured into, ice does not. A liquid is easily manipulated into virtually any shape; however, if its phase is changed into a solid, its shape remains fixed as long as its temperature remains constant. This is the primary reason people use liquid metals, for example, to cast tools, pans, and other objects.

Gases expand to fill whatever container they are placed in. They have both an indefinite shape and an indefinite volume. This is one reason atmospheric gases mix so readily and are found in nearly uniform concentrations throughout the world.

Reading Time _____

Recalling Facts

1. Any material that occupies space and has mass is classified as
   - a. matter.
   - b. an atom.
   - c. an element.

2. At room temperature, iron is a
   - a. liquid.
   - b. solid.
   - c. gas.

3. A synonym for *definite* is
   - a. constant.
   - b. expanding.
   - c. variable.

4. The temperature at which a solid becomes a liquid is known as the
   - a. eutectic point.
   - b. boiling point.
   - c. melting point.

5. The type of phase with an indefinite shape but a definite volume is
   - a. liquid.
   - b. gas.
   - c. solid.

Understanding Ideas

6. The article suggests that different forms of matter have
   - a. the same melting point.
   - b. melting points above room temperature.
   - c. different melting points.

7. At –20° C (-4° F), water exists in its _____ phase.
   - a. liquid
   - b. solid
   - c. gaseous

8. An advantage to using liquid metal to form different-sized nails is its
   - a. hardness.
   - b. ability to change shape.
   - c. ease of use.

9. The article suggests that atmospheric gases mix because
   - a. gases tend to expand easily.
   - b. gases are mixed to begin with.
   - c. the gases are attracted to one another.

10. If a given material has a melting point of 100° C (212° F), that material is not
    - a. a solid at room temperature.
    - b. water.
    - c. a liquid when the temperature is 102° C (216° F).

13 B How Does Temperature Influence Matter?

Matter can exist as a solid, liquid, or gas. The phase largely depends on temperature. Although it may not be apparent, temperature is actually a measure of the average speed, or kinetic energy, of the particles within matter. Therefore, to convert from one phase to another, we simply manipulate the temperature while maintaining a constant pressure; this increases or decreases the speed of the individual particles, called molecules.

The slowest moving molecules exist in the solid phase. Here they are tightly bound to one another and actually appear to have no movement. For example, water molecules in solid ice have limited motion, but to us they appear stationary.

Liquid molecules move faster than solid molecules but slower than gas molecules. Liquid molecules are able to move somewhat freely, as evidenced by their ability to "spread out," or occupy a variety of containers, depending on where they are placed.

To visualize how temperature, kinetic energy, and phase change are related, consider what happens when water is poured into a pot and slowly heated. As heat enters the pot, both the temperature of the water and the speed of the molecules increase. In fact, looking at the bottom of the pot, one can actually see the molecules begin to move more rapidly as some of the liquid is converted into gas and the gas rises to the surface as boiling bubbles.

1. **Recognizing Words in Context**

   Find the word *kinetic* in the passage. One definition below is closest to the meaning of that word. One definition has the opposite or nearly opposite meaning. The remaining definition has a completely different meaning. Label the definitions C for *closest*, O for *opposite or nearly opposite*, and D for *different*.

   _____ a. remaining still
   _____ b. slowly melting
   _____ c. resulting from motion

2. **Distinguishing Fact from Opinion**

   Two of the statements below present *facts*, which can be proved correct. The other statement is an *opinion*, which expresses someone's thoughts or beliefs. Label the statements F for *fact* and O for *opinion*.

   _____ a. Matter can exist in one of three forms.
   _____ b. Water provides the best examples of the properties of a liquid.
   _____ c. Solid molecules move slower than gaseous molecules.

3. **Keeping Events in Order**

   Label the statements below 1, 2, and 3 to show the order in which the events happen.

   _____ a. The temperature of the water and the speed of the molecules increase.

   _____ b. Water is put into a pot, and heat is applied.

   _____ c. Liquid is converted into gas as all of the water turns into steam.

4. **Making Correct Inferences**

   Two of the statements below are correct *inferences*, or reasonable guesses. They are based on information in the passage. The other statement is an incorrect, or faulty, inference. Label the statements C for *correct* inference and F for *faulty* inference.

   _____ a. Phase changes occur only for water and other common substances we use every day.

   _____ b. Phase changes occur often in nature.

   _____ c. As temperature increases, molecular motion increases.

5. **Understanding Main Ideas**

   One of the statements below expresses the main idea of the passage. One statement is too general, or too broad. The other explains only part of the passage; it is too narrow. Label the statements M for *main idea*, B for *too broad*, and N for *too narrow*.

   _____ a. Matter can exist in different forms.

   _____ b. Phase change occurs as a result of changes in the temperature and the speed of the molecules within a system.

   _____ c. The slowest moving molecules exist in the solid phase.

Correct Answers, Part A _____

Correct Answers, Part B _____

Total Correct Answers _____

14 A The Beneficial Garter Snake

Many people have an instinctive fear of snakes. Although some snakes are quite deadly, most pose little or no threat whatsoever, preferring to be left alone. Some snakes are even beneficial. Most biologists speculate that snakes only strike humans in self-defense. Even snakes that spit a fine mist of venom in the eyes of people do so only when threatened, and they never spit to kill.

Typically, humans are not aware they are living in an area inhabited by snakes. One snake that humans are often unaware of is the common garter snake. In the United States, there are 12 species of garter snakes. Garter snakes can be found in wilderness regions such as grasslands, forests, or marshlands or in parts of urban regions such as parks or backyards. Depending on the type, garter snakes can be either land-dwelling or aquatic creatures. They measure up to 76 centimeters (30 inches) long, though some varieties are much shorter. Unlike most other snake species, female garter snakes give birth to live young.

Regardless of the individual species, almost all garter snakes have stripes. They are well camouflaged; their colors allow them to blend into their natural habitat, giving them an advantage when hunting for food. Garter snakes use their sense of sight and their ability to detect vibrations in the ground to locate their prey.

Garter snakes are carnivorous animals. Their diet ranges from leeches, fish, and amphibians to small mammals and birds. They will not attack people unless they are trapped. Garter snakes swallow their prey whole. Unlike constrictors, which strangle their prey before consuming it, garter snakes quickly snatch animals and hold them in place while devouring them.

Garter snakes are actually quite efficient predators and indirectly benefit people through their hunting. They do this by consuming animals that harm or destroy human property. For example, garter snakes feed on leeches, which suck blood from humans, and on slugs, which destroy vegetation. Larger garter snakes eat small mammals—such as rabbits—that destroy large amounts of valuable farm crops.

Garter snakes also benefit humans by eating animals that pose a risk to human health. Rats and mice are an important part of some garter snakes' diet. By eliminating the rodents that carry disease and damage property, garter snakes not only help eliminate pests that may carry bacteria or other contaminants, they also help control the spread of contagious diseases.

Reading Time _____

Recalling Facts

1. There are 12 known species of garter snakes in
   - ❑ a. Canada.
   - ❑ b. the United States.
   - ❑ c. Mexico.

2. Garter snakes eat various kinds of
   - ❑ a. animals.
   - ❑ b. plants.
   - ❑ c. bacteria.

3. Garter snakes hunt by
   - ❑ a. constricting their prey.
   - ❑ b. stunning and holding their prey.
   - ❑ c. using venom to kill their prey.

4. Snakes that spray a fine mist of venom usually do so when
   - ❑ a. defending themselves.
   - ❑ b. hunting for food.
   - ❑ c. searching for shelter.

5. Garter snakes hunt by detecting vibrations in the
   - ❑ a. air.
   - ❑ b. trees.
   - ❑ c. ground.

Understanding Ideas

6. According to the article, garter snakes help people by eliminating animals that
   - ❑ a. spread contamination or cause disease.
   - ❑ b. eat humans.
   - ❑ c. threaten household pets.

7. Garter snakes differ from most other snakes in that they
   - ❑ a. use a mild form of poison.
   - ❑ b. swallow their prey whole.
   - ❑ c. do not lay eggs.

8. All of the following are considered the prey of garter snakes *except*
   - ❑ a. rats.
   - ❑ b. plants.
   - ❑ c. slugs.

9. One can conclude that garter snakes pose
   - ❑ a. little or no risk to humans.
   - ❑ b. a high level of risk to humans.
   - ❑ c. a risk to every species within the regions they inhabit.

10. The article suggests that a well-camouflaged animal has an advantage when hunting because other animals
    - ❑ a. may see the animal but think it is harmless.
    - ❑ b. may not hear the animal coming toward it.
    - ❑ c. may not see the animal or detect its presence.

14 B Snakebites and Antivenin

Every year thousands of people die from the venom of poisonous snakes. It is estimated that 50,000 to 100,000 deaths per year are caused by snakebites. Most of these deaths occur in other countries. India has one of the highest rates in the world. In India alone, an estimated 10,000 to 50,000 deaths per year occur from snakebites, most of these from deadly cobras and vipers.

Treatment for poisonous snakebites requires the administration of appropriate antivenin. Each snake species has a specific type of antivenin that works to counteract the effects of the poison. If bitten by a snake, a person should seek medical treatment immediately, before the onset of symptoms. Many people die because they live in rural areas that are far from hospitals and clinics. Others die because they live in developing countries and cannot afford to buy antivenin, which can cost hundreds of dollars per dose. Many deaths also occur in areas with outdated and ineffective antivenin.

In North America, the dominant poisonous snake is the rattlesnake. Although this snake is responsible for about 5,000 venomous snakebites per year, only 10 to 15 deaths result. Fortunately for people living in North America, medical treatment for snakebites is almost always readily available, inexpensive, and effective.

1. **Recognizing Words in Context**
   Find the word *counteract* in the passage. One definition below is closest to the meaning of that word. One definition has the opposite or nearly opposite meaning. The remaining definition has a completely different meaning. Label the definitions C for *closest*, O for *opposite or nearly opposite*, and D for *different*.
   _____ a. work against
   _____ b. dramatize
   _____ c. strengthen

2. **Distinguishing Fact from Opinion**
   Two of the statements below present *facts*, which can be proved correct. The other statement is an *opinion*, which expresses someone's thoughts or beliefs. Label the statements F for *fact* and O for *opinion*.
   _____ a. Many people die from poisonous snakebites.
   _____ b. Antivenin is an effective treatment for many poisonous snakebites.
   _____ c. India's wilderness is more dangerous than any other country's.

3. **Keeping Events in Order**

   Label the statements below 1, 2, and 3 to show the order in which the events happen.

   _____ a. A person is bitten by a venomous snake.

   _____ b. Antivenin is administered.

   _____ c. Poison from the snake enters a person's bloodstream.

4. **Making Correct Inferences**

   Two of the statements below are correct *inferences,* or reasonable guesses. They are based on information in the passage. The other statement is an incorrect, or faulty, inference. Label the statements C for *correct* inference and F for *faulty* inference.

   _____ a. Every kind of snake venom has an effective antivenin.

   _____ b. Some regions have more poisonous snakes than others.

   _____ c. Many people who receive antivenin survive.

5. **Understanding Main Ideas**

   One of the statements below expresses the main idea of the passage. One statement is too general, or too broad. The other explains only part of the passage; it is too narrow. Label the statements M for *main idea*, B for *too broad,* and N for *too narrow.*

   _____ a. Many poisonous snakes in North America are rattlesnakes.

   _____ b. Antivenin is used to treat poisonous snakebites.

   _____ c. Some snakes are poisonous.

Correct Answers, Part A _____

Correct Answers, Part B _____

Total Correct Answers _____

15   A   Avoiding a Water Crisis

Water is one of the most abundant natural resources on Earth. Unfortunately, most of it is not available for human use. Freshwater represents a mere 3 percent of Earth's water supply, yet we seem to take water for granted and assume there is an endless supply. In some parts of the world, there is a severe water shortage, and this problem will probably spread to other areas. Water is necessary for our survival, so we must take steps to ensure its continued availability. If not, we may someday find ourselves facing a shortage.

Water is essential to supporting life on Earth. Plants and animals alike need water for basic biological functions. The first human civilizations emerged alongside rivers and in areas with predictable rainfall. A reliable supply of water allowed the people to grow crops. As populations grew, they expanded only as far as the water supply would allow. Soon large civilizations emerged by developing well-engineered systems for transporting water throughout the region.

The demand for water increased during the Industrial Revolution. Despite many advances in education and technology, however, people failed to see how limited the quantity of water really was. From 1900 to 1975, the United States population increased fourfold, but our consumption of water increased tenfold. This changed in the late 1970s when people began to realize freshwater was limited and they started to question our wasteful use of it. As news of the looming water shortage spread and conservation efforts gained in popularity, the need for a new water policy emerged.

Among these conservation efforts were the development of water-saving toilets, the engineering of leakproof pipes, and the building of dams. Water-saving toilets have accounted for a huge savings in water. In 1992 Congress enacted a law requiring new homes to use water-saving toilets. By doing so, we use almost 75 percent less water with each flush.

Another solution to saving water involves developing better pipes. As much as 20 percent of the water piped through our cities is lost before it reaches its destination. Although this problem is more common in poorer countries, we can share our technology with them to ensure water is conserved for everyone's use.

Finally, building dams helps conserve water for irrigating crops. This method of conserving water is controversial, however, because dams disrupt the habitat of some animals and kill off large numbers of a species.

Reading Time _____

Recalling Facts

1. From 1900 to 1975, the U.S. population increased fourfold while the use of water increased
   - a. fivefold.
   - b. tenfold.
   - c. twentyfold.

2. Of all the water on Earth, freshwater represents approximately
   - a. 15 percent.
   - b. 6 percent.
   - c. 3 percent.

3. One solution for saving water was the introduction of
   - a. dishwashing machines.
   - b. water-saving toilets.
   - c. newly designed well systems.

4. Plants and animals need water for
   - a. basic life functions.
   - b. hibernation.
   - c. irrigation.

5. Water is used to help
   - a. freshwater ecosystems.
   - b. city modernization.
   - c. irrigate arid regions.

Understanding Ideas

6. It can be inferred from the article that water within pipes is lost because of
   - a. leakage.
   - b. widespread waste.
   - c. poorly engineered dams.

7. Dams are probably built in arid regions to help maintain
   - a. flood control.
   - b. a constant supply of water.
   - c. steady rainfall.

8. The article suggests that building dams threatens aquatic ecosystems by
   - a. forcing people to move.
   - b. altering the balance of plant and animal life within those regions.
   - c. irrigating deserts.

9. About 97 percent of the world's water supply is
   - a. salt water.
   - b. contaminated.
   - c. locked up in the polar icecaps.

10. In the late 1970s, people probably became more aware of the water shortage issue because
    - a. large areas of the United States turned into desert.
    - b. people did not care about the environment until then.
    - c. people started to receive more information about it.

15 B Keeping Drinking Water Clean and Safe

Water is essential to our survival. It makes up approximately 70 percent of our bodies and is required for many bodily functions. Humans must ingest an average of 2 liters (35 ounces) of water a day to maintain their health; therefore, few resources are as precious as clean and safe drinking water. Despite its obvious importance, the supply and safety of our drinking water is something we take for granted. Without strict standards, our health could be jeopardized.

In 1972, Congress passed the Clean Water Act. This act established minimum safety standards for drinking water. Before this time, water from natural reservoirs, such as rivers, was often contaminated with both living organisms and heavy metals. These metals often resulted from the careless disposal of industrial waste. Frequently this meant dumping the waste in rivers. People living downstream from these areas sometimes became ill as a result of drinking contaminated water.

Currently, companies have very strict standards for disposing of waste. Various treatment methods are in place to assure the safety of our freshwater supply. Among the techniques used in the treatment of water are filtration to remove bulk matter and chlorination to kill living organisms. The specific type of treatment differs according to the source of the water, but all water is now tested and must meet strict safety standards before it is judged suitable for human consumption or utilization.

1. **Recognizing Words in Context**
   Find the word *consumption* in the passage. One definition below is closest to the meaning of that word. One definition has the opposite or nearly opposite meaning. The remaining definition has a completely different meaning. Label the definitions C for *closest,* O for *opposite or nearly opposite,* and D for *different.*
   _____ a. filtration
   _____ b. use
   _____ c. waste

2. **Distinguishing Fact from Opinion**
   Two of the statements below present *facts,* which can be proved correct. The other statement is an *opinion,* which expresses someone's thoughts or beliefs. Label the statements F for *fact* and O for *opinion.*
   _____ a. Conserving fresh drinking water is one of the most important environmental issues.
   _____ b. The process of chlorination kills living organisms.
   _____ c. Water is essential to our survival.

3. **Keeping Events in Order**
Label the statements below 1, 2, and 3 to show the order in which the events happened.

_____ a. Tests are done to ensure the safety of freshwater.

_____ b. The Clean Water Act was passed.

_____ c. Water was contaminated with living organisms and heavy metals.

4. **Making Correct Inferences**
Two of the statements below are correct *inferences,* or reasonable guesses. They are based on information in the passage. The other statement is an incorrect, or faulty, inference. Label the statements C for *correct* inference and F for *faulty* inference.

_____ a. Humans can jeopardize their health by ingesting less than two liters of water per day.

_____ b. Filtration and chlorination improve water quality.

_____ c. Water would not be safe to drink if it were not for the Clean Water Act.

5. **Understanding Main Ideas**
One of the statements below expresses the main idea of the passage. One statement is too general, or too broad. The other explains only part of the passage; it is too narrow. Label the statements M for *main idea*, B for *too broad,* and N for *too narrow.*

_____ a. The Clean Water Act helps keep our water safe to drink.

_____ b. Public awareness, legislation, and new treatment methods have helped ensure the quality of our drinking water.

_____ c. Pollution threatens our water and air.

Correct Answers, Part A _____

Correct Answers, Part B _____

Total Correct Answers _____

16 A   The World of Dinosaurs

About 140 million years ago, dinosaurs dominated Earth. No modern land-dwelling animal can compare with the dinosaur when it comes to sheer size. The largest dinosaurs grew to lengths of 45 meters (150 feet) and weighed nearly 80 tons. Many of these amazing creatures were quick, agile, cunning, and territorial. They often hunted in pairs or groups. Although it is difficult to determine the exact nature of these animals, scientists have pieced together clues from their fossil remains. In fact, recent fossil finds have yielded exciting new information about dinosaurs and have radically changed our perception of them.

The word *dinosaur* comes from Greek words meaning "monstrous lizard." Dinosaurs made their first appearance in the Mesozoic era, which began about 250 million years ago. This era is often referred to as the Age of Dinosaurs. It marked a time of great geologic and evolutionary change in the history of Earth. New mountains formed throughout the world; plant and insect species began to flourish on land, and reptiles—the first animals to live on land—evolved.

Dinosaurs lived in a variety of settings, from forests and swamplands to oceans. Although some dinosaurs were carnivores, or meat eaters, some were not. They survived on the abundant plant life that existed at the time. One of the largest and most fearsome meat-eating dinosaurs was the *Tyrannosaurus Rex*.

Reptiles and birds flourished during the Mesozoic era. One of the greatest controversies in paleontology, the study of fossils, centers on whether dinosaurs are more like reptiles or more like birds.

The extinction of dinosaurs is one of the great scientific mysteries. How could animals that were so dominant simply disappear from Earth? Many theories have developed to explain their extinction. Most scientists now think a large asteroid hit Earth at the end of the Mesozoic era, causing huge clouds of dust to block the Sun. Without sunlight, green plants died quickly. Then many plant-eating animals, called herbivores, died. Subsequently large carnivores, which fed on herbivores, also died.

The asteroid theory goes on to speculate that these darkened clouds sent temperatures on Earth to levels below freezing for a period of six to twelve months. The cold temperatures further contributed to the extinction of dinosaurs, allowing only small animals with fur, or mammals, to survive. Although we may never be certain why dinosaurs disappeared, clearly our fascination with these creatures will never end.

Reading Time _____

Recalling Facts

1. *Dinosaur* comes from Greek words meaning
   - ❏ a. vicious creature.
   - ❏ b. monstrous lizard.
   - ❏ c. giant reptile.

2. The Mesozoic era is also known as the
   - ❏ a. Age of Reptiles.
   - ❏ b. Age of Carnivores.
   - ❏ c. Age of Dinosaurs.

3. Animals that eat meat are called
   - ❏ a. herbivores.
   - ❏ b. carnivores.
   - ❏ c. endothermic.

4. According to one theory, dinosaurs became extinct because
   - ❏ a. an asteroid hit the Earth.
   - ❏ b. mammals replaced them.
   - ❏ c. they killed one another off.

5. Scientists are debating whether dinosaurs are more similar to reptiles or to
   - ❏ a. lizards.
   - ❏ b. mammals.
   - ❏ c. birds.

Understanding Ideas

6. The *Tyrannosaurus Rex* probably is considered the most frightening dinosaur of them all because
   - ❏ a. everyone knows it was the most powerful dinosaur that existed.
   - ❏ b. paleontologists have found more of its fossils than of any other kind of dinosaur.
   - ❏ c. it is the most well-known carnivorous dinosaur.

7. It is possible to conclude from the article that many dinosaurs were at the top of the
   - ❏ a. food chain.
   - ❏ b. mountain ranges.
   - ❏ c. evolutionary scale.

8. Some scientists believe dinosaurs became extinct at the end of the Mesozoic era because
   - ❏ a. Earth became extremely hot.
   - ❏ b. no dinosaur fossils have been found since the Mesozoic era.
   - ❏ c. green plants died.

9. What might be another common explanation for the extinction of dinosaurs?
   - ❏ a. gradual climate changes
   - ❏ b. hunting by humans
   - ❏ c. pollution of air and water

10. If an asteroid were to hit Earth today, humans would have trouble surviving because of
    - ❏ a. the destruction of the oceans.
    - ❏ b. the loss of sunlight due to clouds of dust.
    - ❏ c. ultraviolet light.

16 B Paleontologist: Fossil Detective

Nothing inspires awe and wonder in young children quite like dinosaurs. Although these creatures dominated Earth millions of years ago, they are now extinct. The sole evidence of their existence is the fossil remains they left behind.

   Paleontology is the study of the plant and animal life that existed millions of years ago. Scientists who study this prehistoric past are called paleontologists. They dig for fossils, and they look for other evidence of organisms that lived during various stages of Earth's history. Fossils are often embedded in sedimentary rock, which can be analyzed to determine when the organisms died. In addition, paleontologists learn about how organisms lived by studying their skeletal remains, their environment, and sometimes even their surviving tissue.

   In fact, paleontologists recently found living bacteria in the gut of a long-deceased dinosaur. This type of bacteria was thought to have become extinct millions of years ago. Probing further, paleontologists found that the dinosaur died of an infection caused by the bacteria. The importance of this is that many modern bacteria, such as the pathogens that cause food poisoning, are very primitive, or basic, in nature. Studying these bacteria might help scientists develop a new range of antibiotic treatments to kill modern bacteria. In this way, paleontologists piece together the past while providing important links to the present.

1. **Recognizing Words in Context**

   Find the word *pathogens* in the passage. One definition below is closest to the meaning of that word. One definition has the opposite or nearly opposite meaning. The remaining definition has a completely different meaning. Label the definitions C for *closest*, O for *opposite or nearly opposite*, and D for *different*.

   _____ a. ancient organisms

   _____ b. harmful organisms

   _____ c. beneficial organisms

2. **Distinguishing Fact from Opinion**

   Two of the statements below present *facts*, which can be proved correct. The other statement is an *opinion*, which expresses someone's thoughts or beliefs. Label the statements F for *fact* and O for *opinion*.

   _____ a. Paleontology is the study of prehistoric life.

   _____ b. Paleontology is an important branch of biology.

   _____ c. Fossils are often embedded in sedimentary rock.

3. **Keeping Events in Order**

   Label the statements below 1, 2, and 3 to show the order in which the events happened.

   _____ a. Paleontologists find living bacteria in dinosaur remains.

   _____ b. Scientists begin working to find antibiotics for the bacteria.

   _____ c. Paleontologists realize that the bacteria are not extinct, as was previously thought.

4. **Making Correct Inferences**

   Two of the statements below are correct *inferences,* or reasonable guesses. They are based on information in the passage. The other statement is an incorrect, or faulty, inference. Label the statements C for *correct* inference and F for *faulty* inference.

   _____ a. Paleontologists use various tools to dig for fossil remains.

   _____ b. All paleontologists prefer to work outdoors.

   _____ c. Some modern bacteria are similar to primitive bacteria.

5. **Understanding Main Ideas**

   One of the statements below expresses the main idea of the passage. One statement is too general, or too broad. The other explains only part of the passage; it is too narrow. Label the statements M for *main idea,* B for *too broad,* and N for *too narrow.*

   _____ a. Paleontologists are scientists.

   _____ b. Paleontologists contribute to science by studying prehistoric life.

   _____ c. Paleontologists sometimes find living organisms.

Correct Answers, Part A _____

Correct Answers, Part B _____

Total Correct Answers _____

17 A Poisonous Plants

Poisonous plants are everywhere. They can be found in homes and yards, in schools and office buildings, and in tropical regions and deserts. Poisonous plants are so abundant that it may be impossible to identify all of the various poisonous plants in an area. So, to ensure safety, special care must be taken with all plants.

Approximately 1 percent of all plants are poisonous to adults, but many more are poisonous to small children and animals. Most poisonous plants are tropical. Tropical plants are often lush and beautiful, and some produce vividly colored flowers. These are precisely the kinds of plants people enjoy having in their homes, and this is where the risk may come in.

Houseplants in particular need to be handled carefully. Houseplants benefit people by filtering some of the air we breathe. Plants do this by converting the carbon dioxide we exhale into oxygen that we inhale. Plants are also thought to trap and absorb some airborne irritants, such as smoke, dust, and pollens. Many people buy expensive machines to filter and purify stale air, but plants do this as well.

Unfortunately many plants also pose a risk to those living with them. Common poisonous plants include amaryllis, azaleas, daffodils, foxglove, irises, mistletoe, oleander, and poinsettias. Some of these are so poisonous that just a small amount can kill a small child or pet. Oleander shrubs, for example, grow under virtually any condition and are found in yards throughout North America. They pose a serious risk to pets that are attracted to their strong scent.

Symptoms of poisoning vary with the type of plant. Foxglove contains a powerful heart stimulant. Eating part of an azalea can cause severe breathing difficulties. A pet that eats daffodil bulbs will become excited and begin to have seizures, and it may even slip into a coma and die.

Many common fruit trees are also poisonous. Their leaves, bark, and seeds can cause a variety of common ailments. Symptoms may be minor or severe, depending on the variety of fruit. Apricot and peach trees can cause vomiting, abdominal pain, and diarrhea. Cherry and apple trees can cause gum inflammation, rapid breathing, and shock. The pits of avocados, cherries, peaches, and plums are extremely poisonous. For all these reasons, people should learn as much as possible about poisonous plants and then do what is necessary to keep themselves and their loved ones from harm.

Reading Time _____

Recalling Facts

1. Houseplants benefit people by
   - a. filtering the air we breathe.
   - b. eliminating skin irritations.
   - c. decreasing blood pressure.

2. Poisonous flowers include
   - a. daffodils.
   - b. nasturtiums.
   - c. roses.

3. Those most at risk of being poisoned by plants are
   - a. homeowners.
   - b. pets and young children.
   - c. seriously ill people and senior citizens.

4. Which fruit does not have a dangerous pit?
   - a. peach
   - b. pear
   - c. avocado

5. Symptoms of poisoning often vary with the
   - a. location of the plant.
   - b. time of year.
   - c. type of plant.

Understanding Ideas

6. According to the article, poisonous plants can be found
   - a. mainly in remote locations.
   - b. virtually everywhere.
   - c. only in North America.

7. It is possible to conclude from the article that poisonous plants are
   - a. difficult to avoid.
   - b. easily avoided.
   - c. not too dangerous.

8. The article suggests that pleasant-smelling flowers are
   - a. never dangerous.
   - b. always beautiful.
   - c. sometimes poisonous.

9. Plants are likely to filter out all of the following *except*
   - a. cigarette smoke.
   - b. water vapor.
   - c. household dust.

10. The severity of poisoning often varies with the
    - a. amount of plant matter ingested.
    - b. location of the poisonous plant.
    - c. type of soil.

17 B Poisonous Mushrooms

Many people enjoy eating mushrooms. Growing abundantly in forests and meadows, mushrooms carry a certain exotic mystique. Unfortunately, as much as people enjoy their taste and exotic nature, mushrooms can also be quite deadly.

There are more than 10,000 species of mushrooms. Of these, relatively few are seriously poisonous, and only a handful are fatal. Given these odds, it seems strange that so many people die from eating poisonous mushrooms. One reason is that some dangerous mushrooms are similar in appearance to tasty mushrooms.

Mushroom collecting is popular because mushrooms grow virtually everywhere. There is no simple rule to distinguish safe mushrooms from poisonous ones, so only mushrooms known to be safe should be eaten. Despite warnings, some people choose to ignore advice and eat unidentified mushrooms. Others carry mushroom guides with them, trying to identify mushrooms as they collect them. The problem is that many of the 10,000 species of mushrooms look so similar they are difficult to distinguish.

If a person eats poisonous mushrooms, the symptoms may appear within minutes or they may take several days. Symptoms may include bloating, vomiting, abdominal cramps, fever, organ failure, coma, and even death. Given the dire consequences of eating the wrong mushrooms, it is better to eat only mushrooms that you are certain are safe.

1. **Recognizing Words in Context**

   Find the word *dire* in the passage. One definition below is closest to the meaning of that word. One definition has the opposite or nearly opposite meaning. The remaining definition has a completely different meaning. Label the definitions C for *closest*, O for *opposite or nearly opposite*, and D for *different*.

   _____ a. favorable

   _____ b. terrible

   _____ c. harmless

2. **Distinguishing Fact from Opinion**

   Two of the statements below present *facts*, which can be proved correct. The other statement is an *opinion*, which expresses someone's thoughts or beliefs. Label the statements F for *fact* and O for *opinion*.

   _____ a. There are more than 10,000 species of mushrooms.

   _____ b. It is dangerous to pick mushrooms and eat them if you are not an expert.

   _____ c. Mushrooms are a delicious ingredient in many recipes.

3. **Keeping Events in Order**

   Label the statements below 1, 2, and 3 to show the order in which the events happen.

   _____ a. The person eats the mushrooms, and nothing happens at first.

   _____ b. Two days later, the person has severe abdominal cramps and fever.

   _____ c. A person gathers mushrooms in the woods.

4. **Making Correct Inferences**

   Two of the statements below are correct *inferences*, or reasonable guesses. They are based on information in the passage. The other statement is an incorrect, or faulty, inference. Label the statements C for *correct* inference and F for *faulty* inference.

   _____ a. The severity of mushroom poisoning varies with the number of mushrooms eaten.

   _____ b. Collecting mushrooms is always unsafe.

   _____ c. Symptoms of mushroom poisoning vary with the type of mushroom eaten.

5. **Understanding Main Ideas**

   One of the statements below expresses the main idea of the passage. One statement is too general, or too broad. The other explains only part of the passage; it is too narrow. Label the statements M for *main idea*, B for *too broad*, and N for *too narrow*.

   _____ a. It is dangerous to eat mushrooms that were not gathered by an expert.

   _____ b. Food poisoning comes from a variety of sources.

   _____ c. Some people use mushroom guides when they collect mushrooms.

Correct Answers, Part A _____

Correct Answers, Part B _____

Total Correct Answers _____

18 A The Electromagnetic Spectrum

There are many types of light, some of which are visible and some of which are invisible. Visible light can be perceived by the human eye. It consists of both artificial and natural light and includes the colors of the rainbow. Most light is invisible, however. Invisible light includes the X-rays used by doctors to provide images of the inside of the body. The scientific name for light is electromagnetic radiation. All types of electromagnetic radiation have the properties of waves.

Wavelength is the distance from one light wave to the next. To visualize differences in wavelengths, consider ocean waves. As ocean waves move, they are close together at times but far apart at other times. Waves close together have short wavelengths, and waves far apart have long wavelengths.

The different varieties of light, which are categorized by their wavelengths, can be shown on a continuous scale called the electromagnetic (EM) spectrum. This EM spectrum is organized into different portions that range from those with shorter wavelengths, such as X-rays, to those with longer wavelengths, such as radio waves.

The human eye can see light only in a very narrow range in the middle of the EM spectrum. Each color has a wavelength that is slightly different from the wavelengths of other colors. The differences are often too small for our eyes to distinguish one wavelength—that is, one color—from another. White light from the Sun is actually a mixture of numerous colors, but it is discernible to the human eye as one color—white.

Humans can distinguish the colors in white light only if some object filters the colors. For example, a rainbow results from the separation of light by a natural filter. This filter is the water vapor that is in the air as the result of rain.

Invisible light also has many interesting features. While invisible light cannot be seen, it can be perceived in various ways. One example is radio waves, or light within the radio portion of the EM spectrum. Radio waves are not seen but are easily converted into acoustic waves that we can hear. Other types of invisible light include infrared light and ultraviolet light. Infrared light often takes the form of heat. Ultraviolet (UV) light includes the harmful rays of the Sun that require people to wear sunscreen when they are outside for a long time.

Reading Time _____

Recalling Facts

1. Another name for light is
   - a. magnetic energy.
   - b. electromagnetic radiation.
   - c. invisible energy.

2. Light that cannot be seen by the human eye is classified as
   - a. invisible light.
   - b. high energy light.
   - c. visible light.

3. The distance from one wave to the next is called the
   - a. frequency.
   - b. photon.
   - c. wavelength.

4. All the following are examples of invisible light *except*
   - a. UV light.
   - b. X-ray light.
   - c. blue light.

5. The type of light used to reveal bone fractures is called
   - a. visible light.
   - b. X-ray light.
   - c. radio waves.

Understanding Ideas

6. According to the article, white light is interpreted as white because
   - a. the human eye cannot identify wavelength.
   - b. the human eye cannot separate its colors.
   - c. the light really is white.

7. The article suggests that some forms of invisible light can be
   - a. complex in nature.
   - b. colorful.
   - c. dangerous to humans.

8. The article suggests that humans can detect the colors in white light only if the light is
   - a. filtered by an object.
   - b. absorbed by an object.
   - c. identified by its wavelength.

9. If the most harmful kinds of light have shorter wavelengths, you can conclude that _____ has a short wavelength
   - a. infrared light
   - b. visible light
   - c. UV light

10. Only reflected light can be seen. Black holes absorb everything around them, including light. This is why black holes cannot be
    - a. seen.
    - b. felt.
    - c. destroyed.

18 B Do Animals See Color?

Almost all people have the ability to distinguish between colors. Many animals, however, do not have this capability. But that does not mean the animals have poor vision. Some see very well in black and white.

To experience color vision, animals must have two different kinds of photoreceptors in their eyes. These photoreceptors are called rods and cones. Rods are used at night to differentiate between levels of brightness, while cones are used in the day to differentiate between colors.

The eyes of many animals have evolved without cones; these animals do not have color vision. Animals that hunt at night, such as coyotes, have a greater need for rods than for cones. To maximize night vision, the eyes of these animals developed rods. This gave them keen night vision but much more limited vision during the day. This explains why some animals exposed to bright light at night—from a car's headlights, for example—seem almost blinded by that light.

Some animals have acute color vision. Many birds that hunt during the day have more cones than humans do; therefore, their color distinction surpasses ours.

Hawks have evolved an even more complex visual system, with a flat lens in front of their retina to focus on faraway objects. A hawk's lens enlarges its field of vision so that images appear larger, sharper, and more colorful, similar to images seen in the spotting scope of a camera lens.

1. **Recognizing Words in Context**

   Find the word *acute* in the passage. One definition below is closest to the meaning of that word. One definition has the opposite or nearly opposite meaning. The remaining definition has a completely different meaning. Label the definitions C for *closest,* O for *opposite or nearly opposite,* and D for *different.*

   _____ a. precise

   _____ b. inaccurate

   _____ c. attractive

2. **Distinguishing Fact from Opinion**

   Two of the statements below present *facts,* which can be proved correct. The other statement is an *opinion,* which expresses someone's thoughts or beliefs. Label the statements F for *fact* and O for *opinion.*

   _____ a. Animals that have color vision have an advantage over those that do not.

   _____ b. The presence of cones in the eyes is needed for color vision.

   _____ c. Humans have both rods and cones.

3. **Keeping Events in Order**

   Label the statements below 1, 2, and 3 to show the order in which the events happen.

   _____ a. The coyote needs to see well at night to hunt.

   _____ b. Coyotes develop acute night vision.

   _____ c. A type of animal called a coyote evolves.

4. **Making Correct Inferences**

   Two of the statements below are correct *inferences,* or reasonable guesses. They are based on information in the passage. The other statement is an incorrect, or faulty, inference. Label the statements C for *correct* inference and F for *faulty* inference.

   _____ a. Hawks have better vision than all other birds.

   _____ b. Hawks benefit from their complex visual system.

   _____ c. Hawks can see snakes better than many animals can.

5. **Understanding Main Ideas**

   One of the statements below expresses the main idea of the passage. One statement is too general, or too broad. The other explains only part of the passage; it is too narrow. Label the statements M for *main idea,* B for *too broad,* and N for *too narrow.*

   _____ a. The eyes of different animals evolved to fit the animals' needs.

   _____ b. Some animals see colors just as humans do.

   _____ c. The eyes of animals are complex structures.

Correct Answers, Part A _____

Correct Answers, Part B _____

Total Correct Answers _____

19 A Isaac Newton's Three Laws of Motion

Isaac Newton was an English scientist who lived from 1642 to 1727. Before Newton, scientists had little understanding of how the forces of nature influenced objects. Newton not only explained how matter responds to forces, he also suggested that all forces are governed by a single set of natural laws. Newton's natural laws provided scientific explanations for many natural occurrences that scientists had previously been unable to explain.

In 1687 Newton revolutionized the field of physics with his book *Principia Mathematica*. In it, he described some of the most fundamental principles of physics, now known as Newton's Three Laws of Motion. These laws, together with Newton's theory of gravity, make up what contemporary physicists call classical physics, or Newtonian physics.

Newton's first law of motion proposes that moving objects continue moving and that stationary objects continue resting, unless an external force alters their movements. Newton used the term *inertia* to describe the tendency of an object to resist a change in motion. He speculated that if nothing external acted upon the motion of an object, the motion would continue indefinitely. To visualize these principles, imagine what happens to a ball dropped from a tall building. Gravity pulls the ball downward, and inertia causes the ball to continue moving down until it hits the ground. Conversely, a stationary rock on the ground will not move unless another force causes it to move.

Newton's second law states that the force exerted by an object is equivalent to the mass of the object multiplied by its acceleration; the equation is force = mass × acceleration. To understand this principle, imagine one person trying to throw a bowling ball across a field and another person trying to throw a soccer ball. Because the bowling ball has a greater mass than the soccer ball, a larger force is required to accelerate the bowling ball to the same speed as the soccer ball. In addition, Newton's second law states that objects accelerate in the same direction as the forces applied to them; thus, the balls move in the direction in which they are thrown.

The third law of motion states that for every action there is an equal and opposite reaction. Therefore, a standing person exerts a force on the floor that is equivalent to the force that the floor exerts on the person. This keeps nature's forces in a state of equilibrium.

Reading Time _____

Recalling Facts

1. Newton's three laws of motion and his theory of gravity form a system of physics called
   - ❏ a. electromagnetism.
   - ❏ b. relativity.
   - ❏ c. classical physics.

2. Newton published his work in a book titled
   - ❏ a. *Newton's Three Laws of Motion.*
   - ❏ b. *Principia Mathematica.*
   - ❏ c. *Inertia and Classical Mechanics.*

3. The tendency for a body to resist change in motion is known as
   - ❏ a. Newton's third law of motion.
   - ❏ b. Newton's theory of gravity.
   - ❏ c. inertia.

4. Mass multiplied by acceleration equals
   - ❏ a. equilibrium.
   - ❏ b. force.
   - ❏ c. gravity.

5. Newton's third law states that for every action there is an equal and opposite
   - ❏ a. reaction.
   - ❏ b. force.
   - ❏ c. velocity.

Understanding Ideas

6. Scientists prior to Newton lacked a sufficient understanding of
   - ❏ a. mechanical equilibrium.
   - ❏ b. physical forces.
   - ❏ c. planetary orbits.

7. The tendency for bodies to resist change suggests that
   - ❏ a. change requires a force.
   - ❏ b. systems resist change.
   - ❏ c. change is spontaneous.

8. It is likely that no scientist prior to Newton developed universal laws of motion because
   - ❏ a. no earlier scientists studied motion.
   - ❏ b. scientists had no interest in such laws.
   - ❏ c. they had different ways of thinking about motion than Newton did.

9. Contemporary scientists are likely to consider Newton's three laws of motion to be
   - ❏ a. basic.
   - ❏ b. revolutionary.
   - ❏ c. ridiculous.

10. A ball that is dropped from a building will continue to fall downward because of
    - ❏ a. velocity and inertia.
    - ❏ b. inertia and gravity.
    - ❏ c. acceleration and centripetal motion.

19 B Laws of Motion at an Amusement Park

Amusement park rides excite people with unexpected twists and falls. These unnerving events are the result of our bodies' undergoing unusual sensations. Humans are used to the laws of physics that govern their movement on Earth under ordinary conditions. Designers of amusement park rides seek to create sensations that the body is not used to. The rides inspire both fear and a rush of adrenaline.

One ride that strikes fear in the hearts of many is the roller coaster. The principles behind roller coaster design are related to experiments by the famous Italian physicist Galileo Galilei. Galileo demonstrated that falling objects accelerate at a rate of 9.8 meters (32 feet) per second for every second of their fall. While humans typically feel weighted down on Earth, there are ways to achieve the sensation of weightlessness. One way is to cause an object to accelerate at a rate equal to the pull of gravity.

Along with the feeling of free-fall on downward slopes comes the perception of being flung at a tangent from a tight curve. This is the result of centrifugal force, which can be likened to the force felt by a rock at the end of a string being swung in the air. When these forces act in unison, riders are treated to the sensation of floating and the thrill of spine-tingling outward acceleration.

1. **Recognizing Words in Context**

    Find the word *tangent* in the passage. One definition below is closest to the meaning of that word. One definition has the opposite or nearly opposite meaning. The remaining definition has a completely different meaning. Label the definitions C for *closest*, O for *opposite or nearly opposite*, and D for *different*.

    _____ a. straight course

    _____ b. wavy line

    _____ c. change in direction

2. **Distinguishing Fact from Opinion**

    Two of the statements below present *facts*, which can be proved correct. The other statement is an *opinion*, which expresses someone's thoughts or beliefs. Label the statements F for *fact* and O for *opinion*.

    _____ a. Roller coasters are the most exciting rides.

    _____ b. Objects with mass have inherent gravity.

    _____ c. The sensation of weightlessness can be achieved on Earth.

3. **Keeping Events in Order**

   Label the statements below 1, 2, and 3 to show the order in which the events happened.

   _____ a. Amusement park roller coasters were created.

   _____ b. Humans were able to experience weightlessness for a small fee.

   _____ c. Galileo determined the rate of acceleration due to gravity.

4. **Making Correct Inferences**

   Two of the statements below are correct *inferences,* or reasonable guesses. They are based on information in the passage. The other statement is an incorrect, or faulty, inference. Label the statements C for *correct* inference and F for *faulty* inference.

   _____ a. Amusement park ride builders use the laws of physics in their work.

   _____ b. Galileo designed many of the earliest roller coasters.

   _____ c. A person can be very heavy and still experience a feeling of weightlessness.

5. **Understanding Main Ideas**

   One of the statements below expresses the main idea of the passage. One statement is too general, or too broad. The other explains only part of the passage; it is too narrow. Label the statements M for *main idea,* B for *too broad,* and N for *too narrow.*

   _____ a. Unusual sensations can create fear in people's minds.

   _____ b. Weightlessness can be felt when riding a roller coaster.

   _____ c. The laws of physics are used to create dynamic and exciting amusement park rides.

   Correct Answers, Part A _____

   Correct Answers, Part B _____

   Total Correct Answers _____

20 A   Using Technology to Predict Weather

Weather is often defined as the condition of Earth's atmosphere. Water, the Sun's heat, and Earth's motion combine to make weather. Predicting weather is difficult because the atmosphere is constantly changing. When weather-related factors combine in surprising ways, severe weather conditions such as rain, thunderstorms, and hurricanes can occur unexpectedly.

Modern meteorologists use technology to create models of atmospheric conditions to help them forecast weather. Among these complex tools are Doppler radar and weather satellites. These tools are linked to a network of computers so that people can not only predict the conditions at one place but also predict where a particular storm is headed and under what conditions it may worsen. Accurate weather forecasts can help people avoid injury or death.

The word *radar* is actually an acronym for *ra*dio *d*etection *a*nd *r*anging. Weather radar systems work by sending out a beam of energy and measuring the amount of energy reflected back. Objects in the air—including clouds, rain, and even birds—will reflect energy. Radar images are color-coded to indicate intensity. The greater the amount of energy coming back, the brighter the radar signal.

Doppler radar measures both the speed and direction of moving objects. These objects include masses of warm or cool air, clouds, and various types of precipitation. An advanced form of Doppler radar called NEXRAD, for *Nex*t Generation Weather *Rad*ar, is an improvement on traditional radar because it scans conditions to a range of 230 kilometers (143 miles) and is sensitive enough to detect the various forms of precipitation: rain, snow, sleet, and hail. As good as NEXRAD is, however, meteorologists must rely on weather satellites to predict weather outside of a 230-kilometer range.

Weather satellites detect weather trends from outside Earth's atmosphere. Satellites have advantages over ground-based detection systems. For one thing, they provide a more detailed view of clouds. In addition, these instruments not only detect clouds but also measure cloud temperature and thickness. Some satellites travel closer to Earth than others, so satellites are able to provide both detailed views of small areas and general views of large regions.

Satellites allow meteorologists to observe conditions above both land and sea. This is important when detecting and tracking storms such as hurricanes, which increase in strength when they are over the ocean. In fact, weather satellites are an important element of advanced warning systems that help to track severe weather and warn local agencies when conditions become dangerous.

Reading Time _____

Recalling Facts

1. The condition of Earth's atmosphere is called
   - ❑ a. a storm.
   - ❑ b. weather.
   - ❑ c. meteorology.

2. The word *radar* stands for
   - ❑ a. radar detection and reflection.
   - ❑ b. radio direction and roving.
   - ❑ c. radio detection and ranging.

3. An advanced form of Doppler radar is called
   - ❑ a. ADVDOP.
   - ❑ b. NEXDOP.
   - ❑ c. NEXRAD.

4. Weather satellites detect weather from
   - ❑ a. the middle part of Earth's atmosphere.
   - ❑ b. above Earth's atmosphere.
   - ❑ c. the upper part of Earth's atmosphere.

5. Weather satellites enable meteorologists to observe weather
   - ❑ a. above land only.
   - ❑ b. above the sea only.
   - ❑ c. above both land and sea.

Understanding Ideas

6. According to the article, weather is often difficult to predict because
   - ❑ a. weather-related factors interact in unpredictable ways.
   - ❑ b. detection systems are inadequate.
   - ❑ c. meteorologists are improperly trained.

7. When meteorologists compare the radar signal for a hurricane with the radar signal for a light rain shower, the hurricane has a
   - ❑ a. weaker radar signal.
   - ❑ b. stronger radar signal.
   - ❑ c. slower-moving radar signal.

8. As a thunderstorm gets stronger, the radar signal gets
   - ❑ a. duller.
   - ❑ b. brighter.
   - ❑ c. smaller.

9. If meteorologists wanted to measure the temperature of clouds they would probably use
   - ❑ a. an advanced Doppler system.
   - ❑ b. a weather satellite.
   - ❑ c. a basic weather radar system.

10. To track a storm 250 kilometers away, a meteorologist must use
    - ❑ a. a weather satellite.
    - ❑ b. regular Doppler radar.
    - ❑ c. advanced Doppler radar.

20 B   Preparing for Hurricanes

Hurricanes are powerful storms that form when warm ocean air is drawn upward and begins to spin. Within a hurricane, winds can travel up to 300 kilometers per hour (185 miles per hour). When hurricanes reach a coastal area, they bring with them destructive winds, high waves, heavy rainfall, and sometimes tornadoes.

In the United States, hurricane season lasts from June 1st to November 30th. Six hurricanes hit the Atlantic Coast in an average year. In 1986, Hurricane Andrew killed more than 60 people, left thousands of people homeless, and caused more than $20 billion in damage, making it the costliest natural disaster in history. Given this level of devastation, it is easy to see why people should prepare for hurricanes, and, if necessary, evacuate when a warning is issued.

To prepare for a hurricane, it is important to get an adequate supply of canned food, bottled water, batteries, plywood, and nails, as well as a battery-powered radio and flashlight, and protective clothing. It is also wise to remove weak tree branches that might fall and cause damage in high winds.

Next, listen to weather information on radio or TV stations. If a hurricane warning is issued, listen for instructions. If told to stay in your home, secure windows with plywood, if there is time, and turn off all electrical appliances. Local authorities may call for people in low-lying areas to evacuate their communities.

1. **Recognizing Words in Context**

    Find the word *devastation* in the passage. One definition below is closest to the meaning of that word. One definition has the opposite or nearly opposite meaning. The remaining definition has a completely different meaning. Label the definitions C for *closest*, O for *opposite or nearly opposite*, and D for *different*.

    _____ a. destruction
    _____ b. expense
    _____ c. restoration

2. **Distinguishing Fact from Opinion**

    Two of the statements below present *facts*, which can be proved correct. The other statement is an *opinion*, which expresses someone's thoughts or beliefs. Label the statements F for *fact* and O for *opinion*.

    _____ a. Hurricane season in the United States is June 1st to November 30th.
    _____ b. Hurricanes are the worst type of natural disaster.
    _____ c. Hurricane Andrew was the costliest natural disaster in history.

3. **Keeping Events in Order**

   Label the statements below 1, 2, and 3 to show the order in which the events happen.

   _____ a. A hurricane reaches a coastal area.

   _____ b. Homes are flooded.

   _____ c. A mass of warm air begins to spin over the ocean.

4. **Making Correct Inferences**

   Two of the statements below are correct *inferences*, or reasonable guesses. They are based on information in the passage. The other statement is an incorrect, or faulty, inference. Label the statements C for *correct* inference and F for *faulty* inference.

   _____ a. Hurricanes rarely occur before May 31st of each year.

   _____ b. By following a few simple rules, everyone can get through hurricane season without damage to their property.

   _____ c. Hurricanes form over oceans.

5. **Understanding Main Ideas**

   One of the statements below expresses the main idea of the passage. One statement is too general, or too broad. The other explains only part of the passage; it is too narrow. Label the statements M for *main idea*, B for *too broad*, and N for *too narrow*.

   _____ a. People can minimize the risk of injury during hurricane season by following a few simple guidelines.

   _____ b. Hurricane season lasts from June 1st to November 30th of each year.

   _____ c. Hurricanes and tornadoes are the most dangerous kinds of storms.

Correct Answers, Part A _____

Correct Answers, Part B _____

Total Correct Answers _____

21 A — Endangered Species

How does a species become extinct? In the past a species would die off when it was unable to adapt to natural changes in its environment. In recent times, however, some species have become extinct because humans caused changes in the animals' environments. During the past 500 years, more than 800 species have become extinct due to human activity. Efforts are being made by wildlife preservationists to slow the extinction rate and thus to prevent the course of evolution from being changed forever.

When animals and plants are unable to adapt to changes in the environment, they become extinct. This process, called natural selection, was first described during the 1800s by Charles Darwin while traveling on an expedition to the Galápagos Islands near South America. According to Darwin, a British scientist, the better an organism adapts to change, the greater its chance for survival. The process of natural selection has occurred gradually over millions of years, allowing each species a chance at adaptation and survival. Sadly, humans have interfered with this process, forcing species to adapt more quickly than they are able.

Human action has forced many animals to exist in unnatural conditions by altering their native habitats. Habitat destruction is one of the greatest causes of animal endangerment and extinction. Cutting down rain forests threatens animals that are dependent on the forests' native plant life for survival. An example of this has occurred in China, where the population of pandas has dwindled to endangered levels because deforestation has eliminated large areas of bamboo, the panda's main source of food.

Hunting has also altered the survival of many species. At the beginning of the 20th century, the Bengal tiger population of India numbered about 40,000. Today there are fewer than 8,000, because they have been hunted by humans to the brink of extinction. Tigers have always been prized for their beautiful coats but have become even more prized because of their use in traditional Chinese medicines. Poachers will often risk their lives to earn as much as $15,000 per tiger.

Currently the number of endangered animal species worldwide totals more than 1,000, and the total for plants is even higher. Conservationists have sought to reduce this number by working with governments to establish approximately 3,500 protected areas for wildlife. Unfortunately, their efforts have not been enough to offset the forces of economic development, which continues to destroy habitats at an alarming rate.

Reading Time _____

Recalling Facts

1. The concept that a species must change and adapt over time to fit its environment and thus avoid extinction is called
   - ❏ a. evolution.
   - ❏ b. natural selection.
   - ❏ c. survival of the fittest.

2. Charles Darwin developed his theory on nature while on an expedition to
   - ❏ a. Great Britain.
   - ❏ b. New Zealand.
   - ❏ c. the Galápagos Islands.

3. One of the greatest causes of species extinction is
   - ❏ a. habitat destruction.
   - ❏ b. a limited supply of freshwater.
   - ❏ c. pollution.

4. Bengal tigers are hunted because they are used in
   - ❏ a. exotic recipes.
   - ❏ b. Chinese medicines.
   - ❏ c. herding smaller animals.

5. During the past 500 years, more than _____ species have become extinct due to human activity.
   - ❏ a. 8,000
   - ❏ b. 40,000
   - ❏ c. 800

Understanding Ideas

6. Humans have interfered in the process of natural selection by
   - ❏ a. killing off hundreds of species through hunting.
   - ❏ b. putting too many animals in zoos.
   - ❏ c. destroying habitats so rapidly that species do not have time to adapt.

7. You can infer that deforestation is devastating to species because it disrupts their
   - ❏ a. food source.
   - ❏ b. areas for hibernation.
   - ❏ c. source of wood.

8. Illegal hunting is also called
   - ❏ a. adaptation.
   - ❏ b. natural selection.
   - ❏ c. poaching.

9. Conservationists are most likely to agree with the following statement:
   - ❏ a. The extinction of species is inevitable.
   - ❏ b. Species extinction will occur but should happen only through natural selection.
   - ❏ c. All species should be saved from extinction.

10. A population of closely related birds with slightly different beaks most likely evolved to adapt for differences in their environment's
    - ❏ a. food supply.
    - ❏ b. nesting materials.
    - ❏ c. predators.

21 B   Mountain Gorillas

The mountain gorillas of central Africa are one of the most endangered species on Earth. Currently there are fewer than 650 in existence. Several factors have contributed to their decline, including loss of habitat, political unrest in central Africa, and poaching. Although the survival of mountain gorillas is still in question, the effort of conservationists has created new hope for these gentle giants.

    Mountain gorillas are the largest of the great apes. They can weigh as much as 225 kilograms (500 pounds). Because of their tremendous size and strength, they are often perceived as dangerous. In reality, mountain gorillas are thought to be the least dangerous of the great apes. In many ways, their large size and relatively docile nature have contributed to their decline.

    During the early 20th century, mountain gorillas were hunted as sport, and their numbers dwindled. In 1925 they became a protected species. But the illegal hunting—or poaching—of the species continued. This condition did not change until 1967, when Dian Fossey, an American zoologist, came to live with these animals and study them. Through her work, she brought worldwide attention to the plight of these gentle creatures, and she protected them from poachers until her death some 20 years later. Although the conservation efforts of Fossey and others have slowed the decline of the mountain gorillas, their long-term survival remains uncertain.

1. **Recognizing Words in Context**

    Find the word *dwindled* in the passage. One definition below is closest to the meaning of that word. One definition has the opposite or nearly opposite meaning. The remaining definition has a completely different meaning. Label the definitions C for *closest,* O for *opposite or nearly opposite,* and D for *different.*

    _____ a. increased

    _____ b. expressed

    _____ c. decreased

2. **Distinguishing Fact from Opinion**

    Two of the statements below present *facts,* which can be proved correct. The other statement is an *opinion,* which expresses someone's thoughts or beliefs. Label the statements F for *fact* and O for *opinion.*

    _____ a. Mountain gorillas are an endangered species.

    _____ b. Mountain gorillas live in the rain forests of central Africa.

    _____ c. Saving mountain gorillas should be a top priority.

3. **Keeping Events in Order**

   Label the statements below 1, 2, and 3 to show the order in which the events happened.

   _____ a. Mountain gorillas became an endangered species.

   _____ b. People first came into contact with mountain gorillas.

   _____ c. The number of mountain gorillas decreased due to hunting and loss of habitat.

4. **Making Correct Inferences**

   Two of the statements below are correct *inferences*, or reasonable guesses. They are based on information in the passage. The other statement is an incorrect, or faulty, inference. Label the statements C for *correct* inference and F for *faulty* inference.

   _____ a. The population of mountain gorillas has decreased as human population has increased.

   _____ b. Mountain gorillas are completely defenseless.

   _____ c. If mountain gorillas are not protected, they may become extinct.

5. **Understanding Main Ideas**

   One of the statements below expresses the main idea of the passage. One statement is too general, or too broad. The other explains only part of the passage; it is too narrow. Label the statements M for *main idea*, B for *too broad*, and N for *too narrow*.

   _____ a. Mountain gorillas live in central Africa.

   _____ b. Mountain gorillas are an endangered species.

   _____ c. Although steps have been taken to protect mountain gorillas, they are still in danger of extinction.

Correct Answers, Part A _____

Correct Answers, Part B _____

Total Correct Answers _____

22 A Radioactivity

In a dark laboratory in Paris, Antoine Henri Becquerel made one of the greatest discoveries in scientific history. The year was 1896, and scientists were only beginning to understand the basic structure of matter. Becquerel was working with a solid material called uranium, testing its reaction under certain conditions. In his first experiment, he surrounded uranium with photographic plates, an early form of film. He placed the uranium in sunlight to see if it would create images on the plates. He noticed that shadows appeared on the plates, suggesting to him that some image was indeed given off by uranium. He thought about what had happened and reasoned that the sun must have caused this effect.

To test his idea, Becquerel decided to take the same uranium and plates, and place them in a dark drawer where sunlight could not reach them. He looked at the plates a few days later and, to his surprise, found similar images on them. This suggested that something in the uranium was creating the images.

Later, Marie Curie, a colleague of Becquerel's, repeated his work and isolated an unknown material capable of creating similar images. She named the material polonium after her native country, Poland. Curie also coined the term *radioactivity* to refer to materials of this nature. Her isolation of polonium officially marked the dawn of the nuclear age.

Since those early experiments, scientists have discovered much about radioactivity. This understanding has led to the use of radioactive materials for many practical purposes. Applications extend well beyond the devastating weapons that people traditionally associate with the term *nuclear*. In fact, radioactivity has helped enrich people's lives in many ways. From their use in nuclear energy to the radioactive dating of fossils and the advances in nuclear medicine, radioactivity has greatly benefited society.

For example, doctors use radioactive liquids to trace the cellular activity of patients, chiefly people with cancer. Because cancer cells grow more quickly than other cells, one type of test involves giving people small doses of harmless radioactive liquids. Then doctors can determine the rate of new cell growth from images observed through a scanning device. If the number of new cells exceeds normal levels, doctors know that the cellular growth is abnormal. This could signal cancer. The use of radioactive materials in medicine is invaluable because it often replaces more invasive and damaging diagnostic methods, such as surgery.

Reading Time _____

Recalling Facts

1. Antoine Henri Becquerel discovered the radioactivity of
   - a. polonium.
   - b. uranium.
   - c. radium.

2. The term *radioactivity* was coined by
   - a. Pierre Curie.
   - b. Marie Curie.
   - c. Antoine Henri Becquerel.

3. Radioactive materials are used for all of the following *except*
   - a. metallic coatings.
   - b. nuclear medicine.
   - c. radioactive dating of fossils.

4. Doctors use radioactive liquids to diagnose
   - a. influenza.
   - b. cancer.
   - c. hepatitis.

5. Polonium was discovered by
   - a. Marie Curie.
   - b. Albert Einstein.
   - c. Antoine Henri Becquerel.

Understanding Ideas

6. Becquerel repeated his experiment in total darkness to be certain that the images on photographic plates had not been produced by
   - a. the uranium itself.
   - b. sunlight.
   - c. radioactivity.

7. Humans should probably regard the discovery of radioactivity as
   - a. outdated.
   - b. inconsequential.
   - c. important.

8. It is possible to conclude from the article that radiation is
   - a. sometimes dangerous.
   - b. never dangerous.
   - c. always dangerous.

9. According to the article, the shadows appearing on Antoine Becquerel's photographic plates were the result of
   - a. photosynthesis.
   - b. radiation.
   - c. polonium.

10. The number of radioactive applications in future years will most likely
    - a. continue to grow.
    - b. decrease.
    - c. stay the same.

22 B Dr. Chien-Shiung Wu and the Law of Parity

Dr. Chien-Shiung Wu was born in China. She began her education by earning a degree in physics. Soon afterward she left China to pursue a Ph.D. at the University of California at Berkeley. There she specialized in a new branch of physics called nuclear physics.

Following her formal education, Dr. Wu went to Columbia University to conduct nuclear-based research. During World War II, she worked on the Manhattan Project, a government-sponsored program to develop the atomic bomb. She invented a method for separating uranium into its two forms, the radioactive form (U-235) and the stable form (U-238). These two forms of uranium were the key materials in the first atomic bombs.

While pursuing her research at Columbia after the war, Dr. Wu completed her most famous work. Two of Dr. Wu's colleagues had proposed a theory that the "law of parity" did not hold true for all radioactive isotopes. This law states that radioactive atoms emit particles evenly in all directions. Dr. Wu agreed with the theory. She believed that particles were sometimes emitted in specific directions.

Using her knowledge of physics, Dr. Wu designed a test to prove the law of parity wrong. She found that a type of cobalt did tend to emit particles in one specific direction. This finding helped correct some misunderstandings that scientists had had about the basic nature of matter.

1. **Recognizing Words in Context**

   Find the word *colleagues* in the passage. One definition below is closest to the meaning of that word. One definition has the opposite or nearly opposite meaning. The remaining definition has a completely different meaning. Label the definitions C for *closest*, O for *opposite or nearly opposite*, and D for *different*.

   _____ a. strangers

   _____ b. co-workers

   _____ c. relatives

2. **Distinguishing Fact from Opinion**

   Two of the statements below present *facts*, which can be proved correct. The other statement is an *opinion*, which expresses someone's thoughts or beliefs. Label the statements F for *fact* and O for *opinion*.

   _____ a. Dr. Wu helped change scientists' views of matter.

   _____ b. Dr. Wu was one of the most brilliant physicists of the 20th century.

   _____ c. Dr. Wu developed a method for separating various forms of uranium.

3. **Keeping Events in Order**

   Label the statements below 1, 2, and 3 to show the order in which the events happened.

   _____ a. Dr. Wu designed a test to prove the law of parity wrong.

   _____ b. Scientists worked on the Manhattan Project.

   _____ c. Dr. Wu studied nuclear physics at the University of California.

4. **Making Correct Inferences**

   Two of the statements below are correct *inferences,* or reasonable guesses. They are based on information in the passage. The other statement is an incorrect, or faulty, inference. Label the statements C for *correct* inference and F for *faulty* inference.

   _____ a. Scientists are now able to separate uranium into various forms.

   _____ b. The "law of parity" is now a scientific law.

   _____ c. Some decaying radioactive matter will emit particles in a specific direction.

5. **Understanding Main Ideas**

   One of the statements below expresses the main idea of the passage. One statement is too general, or too broad. The other explains only part of the passage; it is too narrow. Label the statements M for *main idea,* B for *too broad,* and N for *too narrow.*

   _____ a. American scientists have played an important role in nuclear research.

   _____ b. Dr. Wu worked on the Manhattan Project.

   _____ c. Dr. Wu made significant contributions to nuclear physics.

Correct Answers, Part A _____

Correct Answers, Part B _____

Total Correct Answers _____

23 A   Animals with Links to the Past

Many living animals bear a strong resemblance to extinct species. We know that animals have evolved over millions of years by adapting to changes in the environment. Animals that were unable to adapt became extinct. Some of the species that exist today show a striking similarity to their predecessors, and many behave in similar ways. Other species have existed for long periods of time without undergoing significant changes.

One species with links to the past is the Asian elephant. Asian elephants are related to an extinct species called the wooly mammoth. Paleontologists have learned a great deal about the wooly mammoth through fossil records. Using fossils and other evidence from the soil, paleontologists piece together clues from the past to determine how prehistoric animals lived.

In the case of wooly mammoths, scientists have quite a bit of information to work with. Wooly mammoths lived in the northern parts of Europe, Asia, and North America. The species was still in existence at the end of the last ice age, and some wooly mammoths were encased in ice after they died. As Earth's climate began to warm, many of the wooly mammoths decomposed when the ice surrounding them melted, but many carcasses in the northernmost regions, where the ice did not melt, remained largely intact. Instead of having just bones to examine, as is the case with most extinct animals, paleontologists have the well-preserved remains of the entire bodies of wooly mammoths. In fact, many of the wooly mammoths were found with partly digested food still in their stomachs, yielding important clues about their diet.

Like elephants, wooly mammoths were herbivores. They ate a wide variety of vegetation, including fir, willow, and alder leaves. Wooly mammoths are thought to have gained access to food in winter by clearing away snow with their tusks.

Scientists are still uncertain how the wooly mammoth became extinct. The wooly mammoth first appeared about 150,000 years ago. As the climate became colder, wooly mammoths adapted by developing tough skin and two layers of hair. At the end of the ice age, however, such adaptation would have proven a disadvantage, and wooly mammoths may have died out as a result of the rapidly warming climate. Another theory is that humans, by then prevalent in those regions, either hunted them to extinction or cleared their habitats to grow crops, forcing wooly mammoths into remote regions where they could not survive.

Reading Time _____

Recalling Facts

1. Wooly mammoths are most closely related to
   - ❏ a. African elephants.
   - ❏ b. Asian elephants.
   - ❏ c. silky mammoths.

2. A species becomes extinct when it
   - ❏ a. becomes encased in ice.
   - ❏ b. fails to adapt to changes in its environment.
   - ❏ c. has only a few living members.

3. Remains of wooly mammoths have been found in the northern regions of
   - ❏ a. Europe, Asia, and North America.
   - ❏ b. India, Africa, and Europe.
   - ❏ c. Antarctica, North America, and Europe.

4. Like modern-day elephants, wooly mammoths were
   - ❏ a. carnivores.
   - ❏ b. herbivores.
   - ❏ c. omnivores.

5. Wooly mammoths first appeared about
   - ❏ a. 150,000 years ago.
   - ❏ b. 10,000 years ago.
   - ❏ c. 50,000 years ago.

Understanding Ideas

6. According to the article, animals can survive major climate changes by
   - ❏ a. traveling thousands of miles in search of different climates.
   - ❏ b. developing physical characteristics suited to the new climate.
   - ❏ c. creating effective shelters.

7. Wooly mammoths would have been most likely to eat
   - ❏ a. elk.
   - ❏ b. fish.
   - ❏ c. pine branches.

8. The biggest advantage to finding the remains of entire mammoths is that
   - ❏ a. they provide more information to scientists.
   - ❏ b. whole animals are easier to work with.
   - ❏ c. decay will be slower.

9. From information in the article, you can infer that elephants
   - ❏ a. use their tusks to hunt prey.
   - ❏ b. scrape away dirt with their tusks to gain access to edible roots.
   - ❏ c. no longer need thick coats of fur.

10. The reason wooly mammoths became extinct
    - ❏ a. may never be known.
    - ❏ b. will be determined for certain within the next few years.
    - ❏ c. has been clearly demonstrated.

23 B — Determining the Age of a Fossil

Fossils are the remains of organisms or the evidence that organisms once existed. Fossils of the actual body parts of living organisms, such as the bones of dinosaurs, are rare. Fossils that provide evidence of once-living organisms are much more common. An example would be an animal track in mud that has dried and turned into rock.

There are many ways paleontologists determine the ages of fossils. One of the simplest ways is to use the principle of superposition. According to this principle, when rock is arranged in layers, older rock lies toward the bottom and younger rock lies toward the top. Therefore, the deeper the fossil is, the older it is.

Another method uses what is called an index fossil. An index fossil is a fossil found in a layer of rock whose age is known. For example, a rock's age might be known if the rock is obviously from a single geologic age. Using this information, paleontologists can determine the relative ages of rock layers above and below the index fossil by assuming a constant rate of superposition.

Certainly there are more complicated methods for aging rocks and fossils. Paleontologists can also use radiocarbon dating, for example. This method involves using a radioactive carbon that appears in tiny amounts almost everywhere. This is a highly accurate method for determining the ages of fossils that are less than 50,000 years old.

1. **Recognizing Words in Context**

   Find the word *relative* in the passage. One definition below is closest to the meaning of that word. One definition has the opposite or nearly opposite meaning. The remaining definition has a completely different meaning. Label the definitions C for *closest,* O for *opposite or nearly opposite,* and D for *different.*

   _____ a. unrelated

   _____ b. comparative

   _____ c. scientific

2. **Distinguishing Fact from Opinion**

   Two of the statements below present *facts,* which can be proved correct. The other statement is an *opinion,* which expresses someone's thoughts or beliefs. Label the statements F for *fact* and O for *opinion.*

   _____ a. Using an index fossil is the best way to age a fossil.

   _____ b. The principle of superposition involves layers of rock.

   _____ c. Fossils are the remains of organisms or evidence of organisms that were once alive.

3. **Keeping Events in Order**

   Label the statements below 1, 2, and 3 to show the order in which the events happen.

   _____ a. An index fossil is found.

   _____ b. Paleontologists study layers of rock in a canyon wall.

   _____ c. The paleontologists determine the age of other fossils in the wall.

4. **Making Correct Inferences**

   Two of the statements below are correct *inferences*, or reasonable guesses. They are based on information in the passage. The other statement is an incorrect, or faulty, inference. Label the statements C for *correct* inference and F for *faulty* inference.

   _____ a. Some methods of determining fossil ages are more accurate than others.

   _____ b. It is possible to determine the exact age of every rock and fossil.

   _____ c. The type of fossil often determines which method is used.

5. **Understanding Main Ideas**

   One of the statements below expresses the main idea of the passage. One statement is too general, or too broad. The other explains only part of the passage; it is too narrow. Label the statements M for *main idea*, B for *too broad*, and N for *too narrow*.

   _____ a. Fossils are an important source of evidence about the past.

   _____ b. An index fossil is a fossil found in an age-determined rock layer.

   _____ c. There are various methods for determining the age of rocks and fossils.

Correct Answers, Part A _____

Correct Answers, Part B _____

Total Correct Answers _____

24 A The Remarkable Brain

The brain is the most amazing part of the human body. Responsible for coordinating every activity of the body, the brain serves as the control center. It receives sensory information from the environment, processes the information, and directs other parts of the body to respond in appropriate ways. Without the brain, humans could not survive. Not only is the brain involved in our decision-making processes, it defines our personality, stores our memories, and makes us who we are.

The average brain weighs only 1.4 kilograms (3 pounds). Although the brain accounts for just 2 to 3 percent of total body weight, it uses more than 20 percent of the body's oxygen. This high oxygen requirement reflects the intense level of activity within the brain.

There are four main parts of the human brain, each responsible for different functions. Two parts of the brain control basic bodily functions. The brain stem is responsible for coordinating such involuntary or automatic activities as breathing, swallowing, digesting food, and pumping blood. The cerebellum is responsible for receiving sensory information from the visual and auditory systems—the eyes and ears. It also controls muscles and joints.

The third part of the brain is called the limbic system. The limbic system controls primal emotions such as love, fear, and anger. Instinctual responses are also under the control of the limbic system. Some experts consider the limbic system to be part of the cerebrum.

The cerebrum is the fourth and most complex part of the brain. The cerebrum processes language, directs motor functions, controls conscious thought and memory associations, and interprets sensory information received by the cerebellum.

The cerebrum is divided into hemispheres, with each half of the cerebrum regulating different functions. The left hemisphere is involved in logical operations and language. The right hemisphere is involved in spatial relations and in music and pattern recognition. Although the hemispheres are connected, current research has shown some people have a dominant left brain or a dominant right brain and actually use one side more than the other.

Research has not shown much difference in intelligence, personality, or creativity associated with hemisphere dominance, but preliminary studies have shown a difference in learning styles. Individuals with dominant left hemispheres seem to learn by processing verbal and analytic information. Individuals with dominant right hemispheres seem to learn through seeing, touching, or actively engaging in activities.

Reading Time _____

Recalling Facts

1. The human brain weighs about
   - a. 1.4 pounds.
   - b. 1.4 kilograms.
   - c. 14 kilograms.

2. The part of the brain controlling breathing and heartbeat is the
   - a. brain stem.
   - b. cerebellum.
   - c. cerebrum.

3. The cerebrum is divided into
   - a. four parts.
   - b. two hemispheres.
   - c. six sections.

4. Instinct is under the control of the
   - a. cerebrum.
   - b. heart.
   - c. limbic system.

5. Of the body's total oxygen requirement, the brain uses
   - a. 5 percent.
   - b. 40 percent.
   - c. 20 percent.

Understanding Ideas

6. Experiments with the cerebrum are most likely to involve
   - a. breathing and swallowing.
   - b. memory and sensory associations.
   - c. anger management.

7. It is likely that brain injury might affect all the following *except*
   - a. muscle coordination.
   - b. breathing.
   - c. hair growth.

8. It is possible to conclude from the article that individuals with dominant right brains might learn more effectively by
   - a. associating facts with music.
   - b. listening to lectures.
   - c. associating facts with logical games.

9. The human brain is still somewhat a mystery because
   - a. it is impossible to study.
   - b. it is difficult to study.
   - c. no one has studied it.

10. You can infer that the part of the brain associated with higher-level thinking is the
    - a. brain stem.
    - b. cerebrum.
    - c. limbic system.

24 B How Does Memory Work?

The human brain is somewhat like a computer. It receives input, processes information by comparing it with existing knowledge, makes a decision, and directs a part of the body to act on this decision. Actually the brain is more like a supercomputer, because it stores billions of pieces of information and processes them in a sophisticated way. This stored information is called memory.

Psychologists classify human memory as either long-term or short-term. Short-term memory includes the sensory perception of objects or ideas. This type of memory is what helps someone recall an event soon after it occurs. For example, when you memorize facts for an exam, you are using short-term memory. You may forget these facts a few days later. If the information is reinforced or processed many times, the information may become part of long-term memory.

Long-term memory can be recalled weeks or years after an event occurs. In addition to reinforcement, events can also enter the long-term memory if they are seen as important. Events that immediately enter long-term memory seem to include those that trigger strong emotions such as love or fear. An example of long-term memory might be strong childhood memories of the taste and smell of a grandmother's cooking. The brain has stored the sensations that were associated with strong positive emotions.

1. **Recognizing Words in Context**

   Find the word *input* in the passage. One definition below is closest to the meaning of that word. One definition has the opposite or nearly opposite meaning. The remaining definition has a completely different meaning. Label the definitions C for *closest*, O for *opposite or nearly opposite*, and D for *different*.

   _____ a. information that is retrieved

   _____ b. information that is complex

   _____ c. information that is entered

2. **Distinguishing Fact from Opinion**

   Two of the statements below present *facts*, which can be proved correct. The other statement is an *opinion*, which expresses someone's thoughts or beliefs. Label the statements F for *fact* and O for *opinion*.

   _____ a. Long-term memory is more valuable than short-term memory.

   _____ b. Events in short-term memory can enter long-term memory.

   _____ c. Events in short-term memory can be forgotten.

3. **Keeping Events in Order**

   Label the statements below 1, 2, and 3 to show the order in which the events happen.

   _____ a. Information about the periodic table enters long-term memory.

   _____ b. The information is reinforced through logical associations with prior knowledge.

   _____ c. Information about the period table enters short-term memory.

4. **Making Correct Inferences**

   Two of the statements below are correct *inferences*, or reasonable guesses. They are based on information in the passage. The other statement is an incorrect, or faulty, inference. Label the statements C for *correct* inference and F for *faulty* inference.

   _____ a. Many events in short-term memory are quickly forgotten.

   _____ b. Almost all events in long-term memory are from childhood.

   _____ c. Human memory is multi-leveled and complex.

5. **Understanding Main Ideas**

   One of the statements below expresses the main idea of the passage. One statement is too general, or too broad. The other explains only part of the passage; it is too narrow. Label the statements M for *main idea*, B for *too broad*, and N for *too narrow*.

   _____ a. Human memory includes short-term memory and long-term memory.

   _____ b. Some events in short-term memory are quickly forgotten.

   _____ c. Humans have various types of memory.

Correct Answers, Part A _____

Correct Answers, Part B _____

Total Correct Answers _____

25 A   Measuring Air Pressure with Barometers

Believe it or not, air exerts pressure on Earth. Pressure is defined as the force that one object places on another object that it is touching. Take a book, for example, and place it on the palm of your hand. Your hand feels the force of the book pressing against it. This force is called pressure. You may not consider air to have weight or to exert pressure, but it does. In fact, air has an average pressure of about 104 kilopascals (15 pounds per square inch). Even though air does not weigh much, we are standing at the bottom of a sea of air 800 kilometers (500 miles) deep! This sea is the atmosphere.

One reason that air pressure is important is that it plays a key role in determining the weather. Changes in air pressure create wind. Wind is simply the flow of air from an area of high pressure to an area of lower pressure. The greater the difference in air pressure, the stronger the wind. In a tornado, for example, a low-lying thundercloud experiences a substantial decrease in pressure toward its center. This change of presence creates a funnel-shaped cloud. If the funnel reaches the surface of Earth, it becomes a tornado.

Air pressure differences can contribute to other extreme weather events, such as hurricanes, cyclones, and thunderstorms. Meteorologists need to know the air pressure at various locations and times to help them make predictions about a severe storm so that they can give people time to prepare for the storm.

The instrument used for measuring air pressure is called a barometer. Two types of barometers are used by meteorologists. Both measure pressure against a standard defined as one atmosphere, which is the pressure of the atmosphere at sea level. The first type of barometer, a mercury barometer, was developed in 1643 by Evangelista Torricelli of Italy. It is a mercury-filled glass cylinder that is closed at the top. If the air pressure is higher than standard pressure, the column of mercury rises; if the pressure is lower than standard pressure, the column drops. When the column drops, it often means that rain is approaching

The other type of barometer is the aneroid barometer. Aneroid barometers use an airtight metal box to measure pressure. When pressure differences are detected, the metal expands or contracts, causing an attached needle to move along a gauge, displaying the exact air pressure.

Reading Time _____

Recalling Facts

1. The force that one object places on an object that it is touching is called
   - a. pressure.
   - b. wind.
   - c. barometric force.

2. Air exerts an average pressure on the ground of about
   - a. 10.4 kilopascals.
   - b. 10.4 pounds per square inch.
   - c. 104 kilopascals.

3. Large differences in air pressure can result in a
   - a. large white cloud.
   - b. barometer.
   - c. storm.

4. An instrument used to measure air pressure is called
   - a. a thermometer.
   - b. a barometer.
   - c. an anometer.

5. Wind is caused by
   - a. differences in air pressure.
   - b. the pressure of the atmosphere on the oceans.
   - c. changes in seasons.

Understanding Ideas

6. If the level of mercury rises in a mercury barometer, air pressure is
   - a. remaining stable.
   - b. increasing.
   - c. decreasing.

7. You can infer from information in the article that a rising column of mercury might mean that
   - a. dangerous winds are possible.
   - b. the temperature is slowly dropping.
   - c. sunny weather is approaching.

8. The article suggests that meteorologists are most concerned with predicting
   - a. seismic activity.
   - b. severe storms.
   - c. ocean water temperatures.

9. A disadvantage of mercury barometers might be that
   - a. mercury thermometers were invented a long time ago.
   - b. mercury is highly poisonous, so these barometers are dangerous if they break.
   - c. very few people are interested in barometers.

10. The pressure underneath an object is more likely to increase as the object's
    - a. weight decreases.
    - b. volume increases.
    - c. weight increases.

25 B Making a Barometer

Barometers are instruments that measure air pressure. An average-to-high air pressure indicates fair weather, while a lower air pressure indicates less-favorable weather conditions. By building a barometer, a person can determine air pressure and make predictions about the weather just as meteorologists do.

Making a barometer is simple and can be done in about 20 minutes. You need the following supplies: a clear narrow glass bottle (such as a ketchup bottle), a clear glass jar, water, food coloring, and a permanent marker. The glass jar must be taller than the narrow glass bottle (without its bottle cap). The narrow bottle is set upside-down inside the jar.

The second step is to fill the jar with enough water so that the water level is 2.5 centimeters (1 inch) above the mouth of the inverted bottle. Next, add food coloring to the water and record the water level by marking the side of the bottle with the permanent marker. This measurement is considered the standard. Because all other pressure recordings will be measured against this mark, the measurement should be done on a clear, sunny day.

Finally, watch the barometer and take measurements at the same time every day. If the water level inside the bottle falls below the standard, then bad weather is more likely.

1. **Recognizing Words in Context**

   Find the word *inverted* in the passage. One definition below is closest to the meaning of that word. One definition has the opposite or nearly opposite meaning. The remaining definition has a completely different meaning. Label the definitions C for *closest*, O for *opposite or nearly opposite,* and D for *different.*

   _____ a. turned over

   _____ b. rotated around

   _____ c. kept upright

2. **Distinguishing Fact from Opinion**

   Two of the statements below present *facts,* which can be proved correct. The other statement is an *opinion,* which expresses someone's thoughts or beliefs. Label the statements F for *fact* and O for *opinion.*

   _____ a. Making a barometer is a good way to learn about air pressure.

   _____ b. Lower air pressure usually indicates unfavorable weather conditions.

   _____ c. Barometers measure air pressure.

3. **Keeping Events in Order**

   Label the statements below 1, 2, and 3 to show the order in which the events happen.

   _____ a. A person makes a barometer.

   _____ b. A thunderstorm begins.

   _____ c. The level of the liquid in the barometer falls.

4. **Making Correct Inferences**

   Two of the statements below are correct *inferences,* or reasonable guesses. They are based on information in the passage. The other statement is an incorrect, or faulty, inference. Label the statements C for *correct* inference and F for *faulty* inference.

   _____ a. The lower the pressure, the lesser the chance of favorable weather conditions.

   _____ b. To get an accurate pressure reading, a person must make sure the bottle does not touch the bottom of the jar.

   _____ c. The higher the pressure, the fewer the thick clouds.

5. **Understanding Main Ideas**

   One of the statements below expresses the main idea of the passage. One statement is too general, or too broad. The other explains only part of the passage; it is too narrow. Label the statements M for *main idea,* B for *too broad,* and N for *too narrow.*

   _____ a. Many kinds of materials can be used to make a barometer.

   _____ b. A barometer can easily be made by following a few simple steps.

   _____ c. Calculating a standard pressure should be done on a clear, sunny day.

Correct Answers, Part A _____

Correct Answers, Part B _____

Total Correct Answers _____

Answer Key

Reading Rate Graph

Comprehension Score Graph

Comprehension Skills Profile Graph

Answer Key

1A	1. b	2. c	3. b	4. c	5. c	6. b	7. c	8. a	9. b	10. b
1B	1. O, D, C	2. F, F, O	3. 2, 1, 3	4. C, F, C	5. B, N, M					
2A	1. b	2. c	3. c	4. b	5. c	6. a	7. b	8. b	9. c	10. a
2B	1. C, D, O	2. F, O, F	3. 2, 1, 3	4. C, F, C	5. B, N, M					
3A	1. c	2. c	3. a	4. b	5. c	6. b	7. b	8. b	9. c	10. b
3B	1. C, D, O	2. O, F, F	3. 1, 3, 2	4. F, C, C	5. M, N, B					
4A	1. a	2. b	3. b	4. b	5. c	6. a	7. a	8. b	9. c	10. b
4B	1. C, O, D	2. F, O, F	3. 3, 1, 2	4. C, C, F	5. M, N, B					
5A	1. a	2. b	3. b	4. c	5. b	6. a	7. a	8. b	9. c	10. a
5B	1. C, D, O	2. F, F, O	3. 1, 3, 2	4. F, C, C	5. B, M, N					
6A	1. b	2. a	3. c	4. a	5. a	6. b	7. b	8. c	9. c	10. b
6B	1. C, D, O	2. F, O, F	3. 1, 2, 3	4. F, C, C	5. N, B, M					
7A	1. C	2. a	3. b	4. a	5. c	6. b	7. c	8. c	9. b	10. b
7B	1. O, D, C	2. O, F, F	3. 2, 1, 3	4. C, F, C	5. B, N, M					
8A	1. b	2. b	3. b	4. c	5. a	6. b	7. b	8. a	9. b	10. b
8B	1. C, D, O	2. F, F, O	3. 2, 3, 1	4. C, F, C	5. B, N, M					
9A	1. a	2. b	3. a	4. b	5. c	6. a	7. c	8. b	9. c	10. b
9B	1. C, O, D	2. O, F, F	3. 1, 3, 2	4. F, C, C	5. M, N, B					
10A	1. b	2. a	3. b	4. a	5. c	6. a	7. a	8. b	9. c	10. b
10B	1. D, C, O	2. F, O, F	3. 3, 2, 1	4. C, F, C	5. B, M, N					
11A	1. a	2. b	3. b	4. a	5. c	6. c	7. b	8. a	9. b	10. a
11B	1. D, O, C	2. O, F, F	3. 2, 3, 1	4. C, F, C	5. M, N, B					
12A	1. c	2. a	3. b	4. a	5. c	6. b	7. a	8. b	9. b	10. c
12B	1. O, C, D	2. O, F, F	3. 1, 2, 3	4. C, F, C	5. B, M, N					
13A	1. a	2. b	3. a	4. c	5. a	6. c	7. b	8. b	9. a	10. b
13B	1. O, D, C	2. F, O, F	3. 2, 1, 3	4. F, C, C	5. B, M, N					

14A	1. b	2. a	3. b	4. a	5. c	6. a	7. c	8. b	9. a	10. c
14B	1. C, D, O	2. F, F, O	3. 1, 3, 2	4. F, C, C	5. N, M, B					
15A	1. b	2. c	3. b	4. a	5. c	6. a	7. b	8. b	9. a	10. c
15B	1. D, C, O	2. O, F, F	3. 3, 2, 1	4. C, C, F	5. N, M, B					
16A	1. b	2. c	3. b	4. a	5. c	6. c	7. a	8. b	9. a	10. b
16B	1. D, C, O	2. F, O, F	3. 1, 3, 2	4. C, F, C	5. B, M, N					
17A	1. a	2. a	3. b	4. b	5. c	6. b	7. a	8. c	9. b	10. a
17B	1. O, C, D	2. F, F, O	3. 2, 3, 1	4. C, F, C	5. M, B, N					
18A	1. b	2. c	3. c	4. c	5. b	6. b	7. c	8. a	9. c	10. a
18B	1. C, O, D	2. O, F, F	3. 1, 2, 3	4. F, C, C	5. M, N, B					
19A	1. c	2. b	3. c	4. b	5. a	6. b	7. a	8. c	9. a	10. b
19B	1. O, D, C	2. O, F, F	3. 2, 3, 1	4. C, F, C	5. B, N, M					
20A	1. b	2. c	3. c	4. b	5. c	6. a	7. b	8. b	9. b	10. a
20B	1. C, D, O	2. F, O, F	3. 2, 3, 1	4. C, F, C	5. M, N, B					
21A	1. b	2. c	3. a	4. b	5. c	6. c	7. a	8. c	9. b	10. a
21B	1. O, D, C	2. F, F, O	3. 3, 1, 2	4. C, F, C	5. N, B, M					
22A	1. b	2. b	3. a	4. b	5. a	6. b	7. c	8. a	9. b	10. a
22B	1. O, C, D	2. F, O, F	3. 3, 2, 1	4. C, F, C	5. B, N, M					
23A	1. b	2. b	3. a	4. b	5. a	6. b	7. c	8. a	9. c	10. a
23B	1. O, C, D	2. O, F, F	3. 2, 1, 3	4. C, F, C	5. B, N, M					
24A	1. b	2. a	3. b	4. c	5. c	6. b	7. c	8. a	9. b	10. b
24B	1. O, D, C	2. O, F, F	3. 3, 2, 1	4. C, F, C	5. M, N, B					
25A	1. a	2. c	3. c	4. b	5. a	6. b	7. c	8. b	9. b	10. c
25B	1. C, D, O	2. O, F, F	3. 1, 3, 2	4. C, C, F	5. B, M, N					

Reading Rate

Put an X on the line above each lesson number to show your reading time and words-per-minute rate for that lesson.

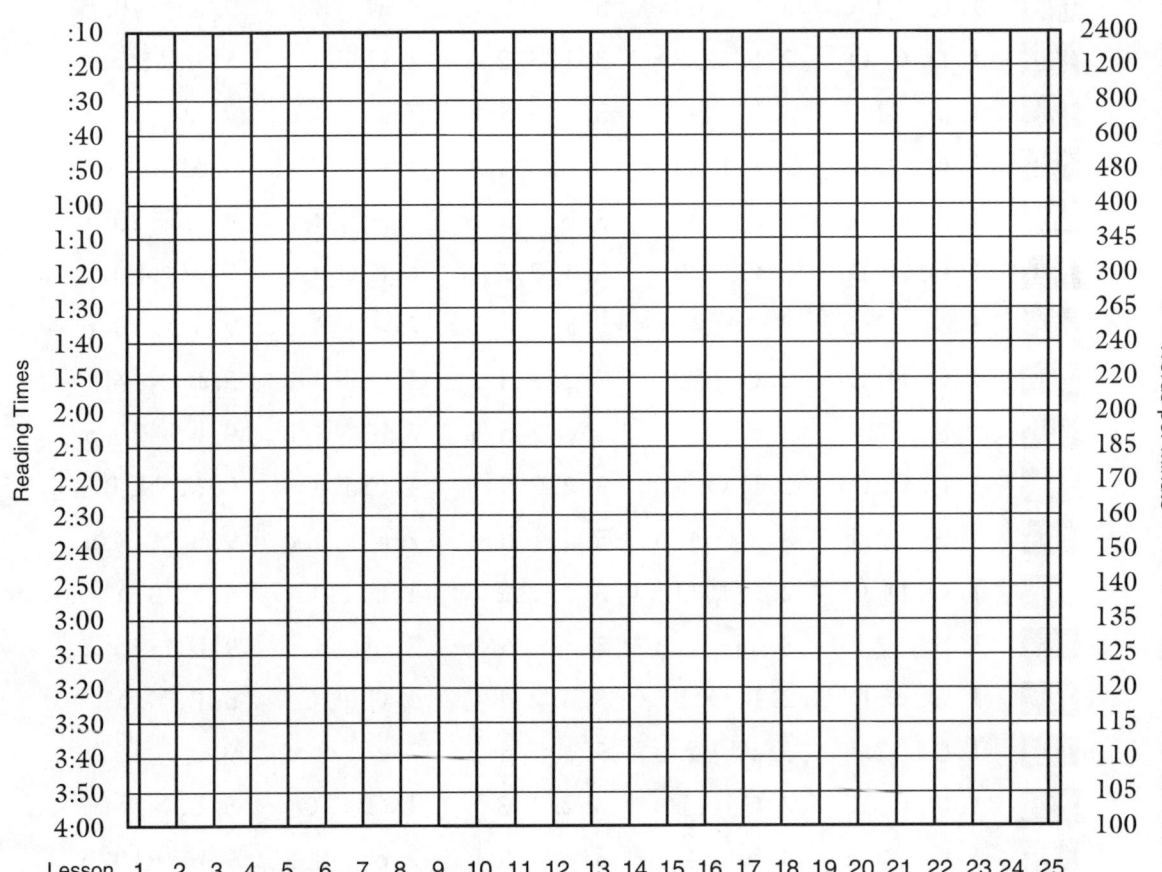

COMPREHENSION SCORE

Put an X on the line above each lesson number to indicate your total correct answers and comprehension score for that lesson.

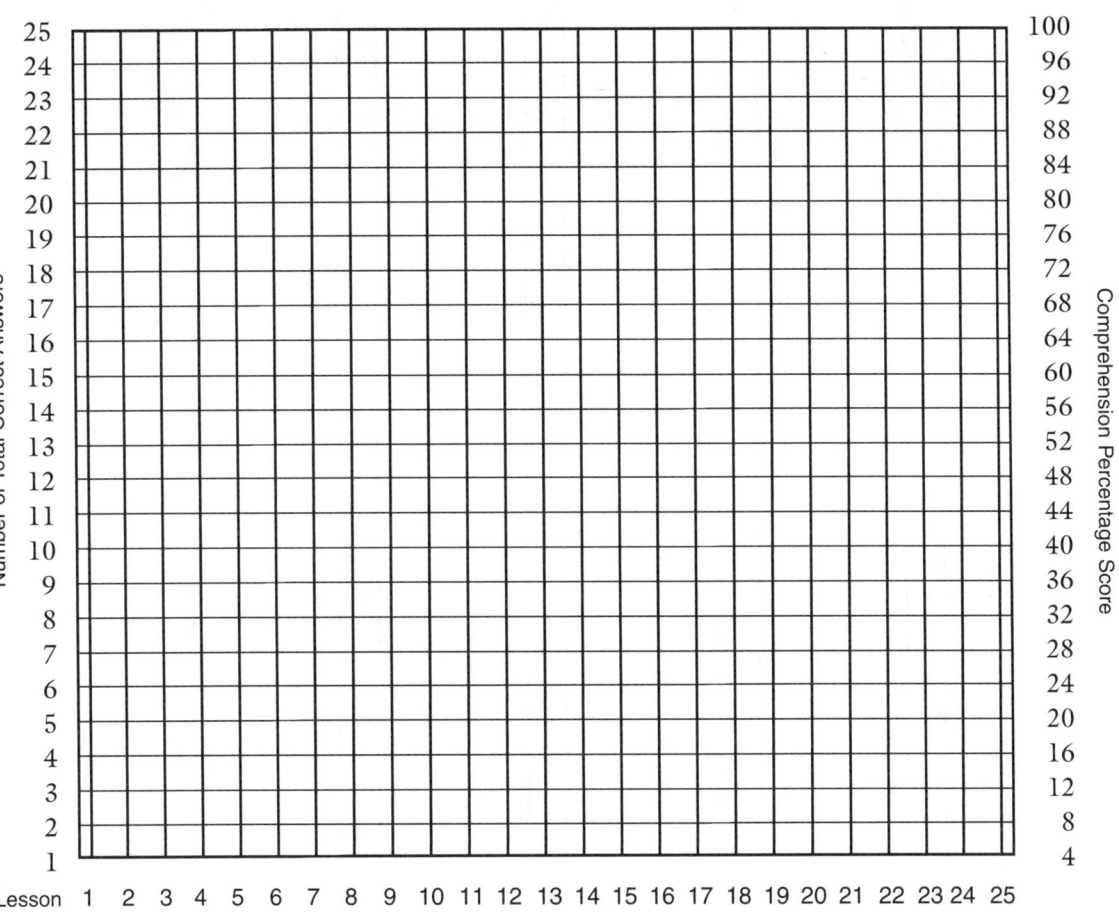

COMPREHENSION SKILLS PROFILE

Put an X in the box above each question type to indicate an incorrect reponse to any part of that question.

Lesson 1
2
3
4
5
6
7
8
9
10
11
12
13
14
15
16
17
18
19
20
21
22
23
24
25

Recognizing Words in Context

Distinguishing Fact from Opinion

Keeping Events in Order

Making Correct Inferences

Understanding Main Ideas